wp13
£3.49

THE LIFE
OF
JOHN DUNCAN

A. Moody Stuart

THE BANNER OF TRUTH TRUST

THE BANNER OF TRUTH TRUST
3 Murrayfield Road, Edinburgh EH12 6EL
PO Box 621, Carlisle, Pennsylvania 17013, USA

*

First published 1872
© *The Banner of Truth Trust 1991*
ISBN 0 85151 608 4

*

Printed and bound in Great Britain
by The Bath Press, Avon

CONTENTS.

CHAPTER IV.

MISSION TO THE JEWS IN HUNGARY.

CHAPTER V.

LIFE IN EDINBURGH.

CHAPTER VI.

HIS MENTAL CHARACTER.

CHAPTER VII.

LEADING MORAL FEATURES.

CHAPTER VIII.

THEOLOGICAL VIEWS.

CHAPTER IX.

VIEWS ON THE CHURCH.

CHAPTER X.

THOUGHTS ON PREACHING.

PUBLISHERS' PREFACE

It has to be a matter for regret that no twentieth-century biography exists of Dr John Duncan, one of the most penetrating and suggestive of all biblical thinkers of the last century. Several reasons probably lie behind the omission. In the first instance, the school of experimental, heart theology which Duncan represented has suffered a major decline since his days, not only in Scotland but across the English-speaking world. Preachers and biographers of his convictions have been few and far between. Another reason, we suspect, is that, in some quarters, a colourful but superficial memory of the man has lingered which has militated against the recognition of his true stature. Duncan was in some respects a man of genius and as with some others belonging to that category he had some notable eccentricities and idiosyncrasies. Too often these were the things which were remembered and talked about – often by his would-be admirers – long after the more important things about him were being forgotten. A few often-repeated anecdotes became a substitute for a real knowledge of his life and thought.

It is certainly not the lack of source material which accounts for the lack of a modern biography. At around the time of Duncan's death three books were published, *Colloquia Peripatetica: Deep-Sea Soundings, Being Notes of Conversations with the late John Duncan*, William Knight, 1870; *Life of the late John Duncan*, David Brown, 1872, which was followed in the same year by this present volume. Two years later in a volume of Duncan's sermons, *In the Pulpit and at the Communion Table*, David Brown added a 'Biographical Supplement' of 153 pages. The diffuse way in which this information was spread, in books which have often been hard to obtain, has increased the need for a new biography. Perhaps such a book will yet appear but in the meantime we have no doubt that the best introduction to the man lies in this work by Alexander Moody Stuart (1809–1898).

Moody Stuart became minister of St Luke's, Edinburgh, in 1835, and in that church R. M. M'Cheyne was among his early hearers. In the next decade, Duncan, then Professor of Hebrew in the New College, became an attender and elder and he remained a close friend of Moody Stuart's for the rest of his life. The truth is that the two men had some marked similarities. While Duncan could say of his minister, 'he knew not a greater master in spiritual analysis', Moody Stuart, writes his biographer, highly valued his elder's opinion 'on all the knottiest points of theology as well as in cases of conscience' (*Alexander Moody Stuart*, Kenneth Moody Stuart, 1899, p. 94). Dr Marcus Dods says of Moody Stuart's memories of his friend that they were 'moulded by the hand of a master into a likeness which must rank among the half-dozen masterpieces of literary portrait painting which our country boasts'.

Such a book as this not only gives us a moving insight into an age that is past but, more importantly, it takes us to convictions which, because they are biblical, lie at the heart of recovery and advance in the church in all ages.

THE PUBLISHERS
June, 1991

CHAPTER I.

HIS EARLIER LIFE.

Oh what a solemn thing it is to be a Man! Made so exalted,
fallen so low, capable of being raised again so high.—J. D.

"THE righteous shall be in everlasting remembrance" was a divine edict often repeated
by our deceased teacher, whose own memory
is fragrant in the hearts of many in Scotland.
By not a few on earth he is still greatly "beloved and longed for," in the hope of "the
coming of our Lord Jesus, and our gathering
together unto Him." To myself he was a
beloved friend and father, to whom I owe a
debt of gratitude which I refrain from expressing, lest my estimate should appear excessive.

In the absence of writings, his many sayings
will preserve his memory, and perhaps even
more effectually. Except for transcribing the
characters of ancient and foreign languages, in
which he took a great pleasure, he had always
an extreme aversion to the use of the pen. As
a student, it was said that his ink used to be
dry in the bottle, and the love of writing did
not grow upon him with years. His own
account of it was, "I never *wrote* a sermon but

3

it made me sick;"[5] and few sicknesses befell him from contact with pen and ink.

HIS BOYHOOD.

Here we are, with the heavens above our heads. What are we? Men. How came we to be men? What is man? How came he to be? and to be as he is? We are on the earth, and the beasts can't ask any questions. The heavens are above us, and the eagles soaring into them can't ask any questions. Man is God's image on earth.—J. D.

John Duncan was born in Aberdeen in 1796. His father was a shoemaker, with his workshop in his own house, but having a good range of customers in his limited sphere : standing by himself alone, John Duncan the elder, a detached boulder of granite, hard and solitary, with none of his kindred near him, or known to his family ; an upright man, walking in the fear of God, strict in his Secession principles, rugged and stern, in family discipline inexorable. His mother's relatives were of a stock of Aberdeenshire farmers, of genial dispositions, and endued with an hereditary taste for the cultivation of the soil ; which led some of them, when living in the town, to lease a field or two in the country outside, that they might mingle with corn and cattle, and might look upon the free face of nature ; she was herself full of human kindness and divine grace. The extremely opposite characters of John and Ann Duncan throw light on the very peculiar character of their only surviving son : the inflexible determination of the father underlying the tenderness of the mother, and the two elements co-existing in a manner rarely paralleled. His mother was taken from him by death when he was five or six years of age. He was a delicate, dreamy, clever, engaging, affectionate, high-spirited, and occasionally passionate boy ; sometimes crying bitterly under the severity of his father's discipline ; sometimes abruptly laughing aloud at the brightness or at the humour of his own thoughts. Having in his own dreamy way lost his Catechism at school, he trembled to face his father, and instead of returning home betook himself to the house of one of his maternal uncles, who welcomed him with the kindly remark : " John Duncan 's over fond o' Solomon's plan ; but I think I 'll manage the boy wanting the rod." Two or three years after his mother's death the vacant place was occupied by an excellent stepmother, of whom he said characteristically, " She has been a most admirable mother—truly *stepping* into the spirit of the relation—to me."

The liking for animals which he found in his uncle's house he retained through life. For nature in general, or for plants, he did not seem to care, although it was one of his favourite sayings, " Consider Jesus Christ, and if you can't consider Christ, consider the lilies of the field how they grow." Yet the flower which he admired was rather the lily as beautified by the words of Jesus than as clothed by its Creator. But he liked animals in themselves, and used to speak of the measure of reason with which they were endowed. " Dogs have a kind of reason ; instinct is just a word for our ignorance. Man is their god, their highest idea of being."

He never judged that he knew the Saviour in his childhood, but he preached on a chair in his uncle's house, and out of a cart to his companions at school; and his cousin said of him : " My father's own religion was so cheerful, and he made it so engaging in the house, that it was scarce possible for the boy to live under his roof without religious impressions. Often when he was in the fields with the family and saw a ship on the sea he said, 'That's the ship that's to carry me to preach to the heathen;' and afterwards, when he was ill, he prayed that God would spare him till he got the red cloak at college." The religious desire and the literary ambition had both deeper meanings than in the lips of a common boy; for he always put forth an unusual energy in following out and attaining any object, great or little, on which he had set his heart. He would take up a poor Jew, would go from one friend to another with the case, and would never cease till he had got the amount he required for him. One afternoon, having called upon a lady on such an errand, he found her just going out, but she offered him what was in her purse; he counted it, found it to be thirty shillings, and said with delight, " That is exactly the sum I needed, and I had given this afternoon to collect it, but now I will go in and play with the children." So also, you went with him to a crowded hall, but stood arrested at the door in despair ; he disengaged himself from your arm, disappeared in the crowd, and wormed himself through till you saw him seated near the speakers. In the great objects of his life again, he was both far-seeing regarding the event, and very resolute and patient for its attainment. As a child he would be a missionary, and as a missionary he spent one of the best and most fruitful portions of his life; as a boy he longed to be a student, he became one through many difficulties, and studied to better purpose than any of his fellows; as a man, he was set on teaching a Hebrew chair, and through a way that he thought not of he occupied that influential position for his last twenty-seven years.

But his boyish hopes for the scarlet gown and the missionary ship were rudely dashed by his father assigning him a stool beside himself, for shoemaking, which in Scotland has often been fertile in hatching a variety of thoughts "supra crepidam," without any startling mishap to the shoes. The lowly place seems to have been taken silently and as under the dread doom of fate, without remonstrance or entreaty. But the distasteful work was constantly marred in his hands, while his tears over his misplaced stitches did little to right what was wrong. In his favourite "linguistics" he showed aptness enough for tracing exactly the various characters of many tongues; if Hebrew or Sanscrit mottoes had been to be inscribed on the shoes, he would have wrought every stitch in its own place with punctilious fidelity; and he was perhaps secretly careless about the marring of his

work, if it might procure for him the coveted
release from the last and the awl.   This it did
at length through his mother's intercession, and
he was sent to the Grammar School.

HIS APOSTASY.

It is a blessed thing that we are not placed amid the grinding and
    wheeling of a great Machine of a universe without guiding
    hand or animating heart.   There is a God, there is a God,
    Jehovah he is the God, Jehovah he is the God.—J. D.

In the University he seems to have had the
characteristics of his later years ; not distinguishing himself in the regular work of the
classes, but labouring hard in his own fitful
way in languages, literature, and philosophy ;
and at the same time showing that affection
for children which he cherished through life.
His mind was naturally inquisitive, far beyond almost all other men's ; and he was
conscious to himself of a very uncommon power
of sifting the subject of his inquiry.   His taste
for languages, with all its keenness, had probably its root in a desire to know them as instru-
ments of thought.   But when he had once
begun to enter into philosophical problems he
must have been carried rapidly toward what he
took for the heart of them, both by a bounding
delight in the effort, and by an insatiable
curiosity for the result.   In his speculations he
cast away the Bible ; and this ground once lost,
he sank down, through unbelief, deism, pantheism, into material atheism, whence there
was no lower depth into which to sink ; deny-
ing the existence of God, of angelic spirit, of

human soul. The man, whom God was about to bring into a more intimate knowledge of Himself than almost any other man of his generation, was suffered for a time to wander to the furthest extreme of alienation.

In his subsequent life he cherished a constant love for the seventy-third Psalm : " But as for me, my feet were almost gone, my steps had well-nigh slipped. . . . How doth God know ? Is there knowledge in the most High ? . . . So foolish was I and ignorant ; I was as a beast before Thee. But God is the Rock (*Heb.*) of my heart, and my portion for ever."—The Rock recalls, in passing, his affection for the hymn, " Rock of Ages, cleft for me," which he held to be by far the first of all uninspired hymns ; he had three threes of hymns, ranked according to their possession of unction, of genius, of rhythm, and this was the first of the first three, combining in the highest degree all these excellencies within itself ; the second being, I think, " There is a fountain filled with blood."—But the seventy-third Psalm, with Asaph's feet all but slipping from the Rock, in doubts regarding the knowledge and the goodness of God, is an experience of which I never saw the slightest trace in him during the forty years of our intercourse ; he betrayed no shadow of a doubt concerning the Bible and its revelation of God in Christ. His continuous love, therefore, for this Psalm must have had its root in the remembrance of his early atheism, and of his redemption out of that deep pit.

In his lowest depth he almost seemed to have

had a tinge of Solomon's thought, " I sought in my heart to lay hold on folly, yet my wisdom remained with me." It was a terrible descent for a youth brought up like him, with so much scriptural knowledge and religious training, with an innate reverence so deep, and a natural conscience so active ; for a time the one half of the man appeared to have so gained the mastery, and so urged its own course, as to make shipwreck of the other.

As the fruit of his philosophic search he discovered a godless humanity ; and stood without belief in the unseen God, without fear, without hope in the world. And what was the humanity that he found, the man without God ? Atheism, in its own nature, exalts man in its attempt to cast God down, and he so far exalted himself. But atheism also naturally magnifies the man whom it has seated on the vacant throne, and glories in that humanity which is the noblest and highest existence of which it has any conception, or in which it has any belief. Not so did John Duncan. He was mortified at his own littleness and the littleness of all humanity. Man without God and without immortality possessed nothing to admire, nothing to interest, nothing to respect, nothing to love. Man was in his eyes a mere animal, which he described to me as like the other beasts, living for nothing higher than going through the degrading sameness of the recurring round of nature's wants and daily supplies. His description was drawn in terms of such force as could have occurred only to a man who

felt himself involved in such a condition. Oh!
how he despised and loathed the Man whom
his philosophy had discovered for itself; the
soulless, godless, apelike man, " born to eat, and
to drink, and to digest, and to die!" When
as a fool he had said in his heart, " There is
no God," there still remained this solitary trace
of " his wisdom remaining with him." At the
same time, also, he never lost his perception of
the difference between the nominal and the
real in religion. " When I was an atheist," he
said once at my table, " I used to feel that if
the Evangelic system were only true it was
worth a man's believing; but even if the Moder-
ate system [of an easy, worldly religion, in
which a man required little to save him beyond a passable character] were true, it was
not worth believing."

Probably his own early lapse into infidelity
rendered him more alive to the fear, which he
often expressed, of an approaching world-wide
struggle with atheism. If the danger arising from
Popery was mentioned in conversation, he would
assent, but never without adding that the great
danger is atheism. Of the Church of Rome he
said, before the meeting of the late Council,—
" The Pope may find that he'll bring down an
old house about his ears.—No doubt many a
devout soul has found its spiritual nourishment
in that Church. Wheat and arsenic, wheat
and arsenic; it all depends on the propor-
tions." But atheism had no redeeming grain
of wheat; and he often repeated his deep impression of a hastening conflict throughout the

world on the foundation of all religion. In speaking of it he did not seem to me to draw any line between the atheism which denies God altogether, and the pantheism which confounds God with the universe, and denies the personal, living God. His words were,—" The great controversy that is coming is about the existence of God ;" and he held that in this controversy physical science can avail nothing, and is not entitled to offer any judgment. " In the nature of things," he said to me, " it is impossible that science can ever discover the existence of God, because science deals with phenomena, and with nothing else. If God were a phenomenon, science might by searching find him out ; but God is not a phenomenon, and science can never discover him."

His mental and spiritual darkness naturally issued in a low moral condition. The joy which he had not in the "answer of a good conscience," he sought to find in the fellowship of companions as thoughtless as himself, regardless of self-restraint, and frequently " running with them into the same excess of riot." Not, however, that he fell into habitual intemperance. The narrative of his life has indeed been sometimes taken in this sense, but this is certainly not the meaning of his biographer ; and when I stated this imputation to his cousin, in whose house he was always on the most intimate footing, her denial was decided : " I never heard of anything of the sort ; he always sat up to all hours of the night, but I never heard of such a charge ; we were ever hearing plenty of faults laid to him, and if that had been one of them we must have heard of it." His walk was quite unbecoming a candidate for the sacred ministry; but except in the way already noticed, and to the extent intimated, his youthful course does not appear to have been stained by vice.

There were two deep elements in his character, good in themselves, which he retained all his life long, and which at this period must have tended strongly both to exaggerate and to exhibit the evil influences that were prevailing over him. He had constitutionally an exuberant joyousness of spirit—not exactly of animal spirit, although that was not wanting, but of natural temperament; and although he was apt to be absorbed in books at home, his natural buoyancy was ever ready to break out in intercourse with his friends. "We like when Mr. Duncan comes to stay with us, he makes everybody in the house so happy," was a remark made in my house when he used to visit me here during his ministry in Glasgow. While it was hard for him to abstain from his subtle word-cutting as with the edge of a razor, he never seemed to care for the kind of wit which consists of a play upon words; but he revelled in humour, and his talk was often enlivened with humorous sayings in their most picturesque dress, and in their original cast of dialect. Even when least expected, his natural joyousness would break through much of a contrary character, and it could not but carry him into extremes when he knew no higher joys than those of earth. His life-long choice of " the pleasures for evermore" was not influenced by any natural disrelish or inaptitude for the enjoyment of this present life, of which he might have said with Solomon, "Who else can hasten thereunto more than I?"

Along with innate cheerfulness he had an intensely social temperament. It was hard to determine which he loved most, solitude or society; or which he disliked most, if he was bent upon the other. You might truly describe him as one of the most unsocial men you ever knew; and you might say still more truly that you never knew a man more intensely social. In company he would take up a book, or would absorb himself in his own thoughts without uttering a word, or seeming to know or to care for any one's presence; and at home he would bury himself in books for days or for weeks. But if you were engaged, and gave him a quiet room and books, he would be quite restless and seemingly incapable of study, and he would scent you out in any part of the house to get you into conversation; so that a friend said of him, "he was instant in season, and specially out of season." This strongly social temperament made his thoughts useful to others, when without it they would have been. lost; but while grace turned this disposition into a lasting good throughout his long life of grace, it was perverted to evil in his student life, when his love of society took the form of a convivial intercourse, of which he afterwards repented.

After studying for two or three years in his

own branch of the Secession Church, he joined the Church of Scotland; and in a very unfit state of mind, with no proper motives, and with no right sense of the seriousness of the transaction, he entered the Divinity Hall in Aberdeen. He was then a member of Dr. Kidd's church, but derived no saving benefit from his ministrations. But few things can be imagined more touching than the filial tenderness, reverence, love, and admiration with which John Duncan regarded Dr. Kidd after his conversion; and I often admired the vivid hues in which he depicted their intercourse. " Young man, will you hold your tongue, and let the Holy Ghost speak ?" were words which he frequently quoted as spoken to him by his pastor, when in reading the Bible to a condemned criminal in his cell he was interspersing it with his own comments.

The Doctor's fiery energy on the one hand, and his lowly tenderness on the other, he used to draw in two companion pictures. The burning fire broke out in a conversation with a Jew, at which Duncan seemed to have been present. The Jew sometimes argued with Dr. Kidd on the evidences of Christianity, and, mistaking the character of the man with whom he was conversing, he ventured one day to speak disparagingly of the Virgin Mary. The Doctor had patience with his arguments against the gospel, but his reproach against Mary was more than he could endure. " Sir," said he, shaking his massive fist in Israel's face, " if you dare to speak evil of the Mother of my Lord, I 'll knock you down." With all his pity and partiality for the Jews, John Duncan was singularly cordial in calling Mary " Blessed among women;" and he rehearsed the threat with a glowing animation and in a sonorous depth of tone, which showed that his heart would not have recoiled from witnessing the blow in retaliation for the offence.

Hastiness in speech was one of Dr. Kidd's infirmities ; and over against this not ignoble burst of anger his friend spoke of his meekness in his own defence in a scene which cannot be drawn in words, because it mainly consisted of silence, but which a painter could have well described in a didactic picture. The youthful and slender disciple, in the tenderness of his early Christian love, was walking along the street with the stately divine of whom men were wont to stand in affectionate awe as he passed along. In conversation the expression " My God" escaped from his lips with seeming want of reverence, and the rashness touched the young man on the apple of his eye. The depth and tenderness of his own reverence are strikingly brought out in one of his letters written a few years later. In the course of a long statement he had introduced one of the names of God or of Christ too early in the sentence, and drawing his pen through it at the instant he introduced it rightly afterwards. But on the margin he writes this note : " I am very sorry for the erasure ; I did it hastily and without thought, but if I had taken time I would have put the word in an enclosure, thus ⌐⌐." The haste of the pen in the one

case was as nothing to the haste of the tongue
in the other, and his heart, so tenderly sensitive to his heavenly Father's honour, was pain-
fully wounded; but he suppressed all expression
of his feelings at the moment. After they had
walked on together till they were about to
part, the youth gently took hold of the father's
hand, and most modestly, without raising his
eyes, recalled his attention to the word: " I
think, Doctor, you said 'My God' a little while
ago." The Doctor looked kindly down on
him and pressed his hand; neither of them
said more, but the loving remonstrance only
awakened an enhanced return of love.

Meanwhile, however, for a number of years,
till the Lord's time had come for opening his
heart to himself, he went on in the light of
his own mind. But in the Divinity Hall he
was impressed with Dr. Mearns's prayers to
the " Great King;" and his cogent reasonings
convinced him intellectually of the existence
of the living God. The gain was to him in-
valuable. " It was Dr. Mearns," he frequently
said to me, " who satisfied me of the existence
of God;" and through life he remembered the
debt with lively gratitude.

But the conviction had been reached by a
logical process, without any more direct mental
perception; rather his reason accepting, than his
mind seeing it. The next stage of light seems
almost to belong to the operation of the Spirit
of God, and to involve on his part a special
resistance in not following it up to spiritual
fruit. It was the breaking in of a light which

B

he looked back upon to the last as an era in his life, and spoke of as a season of indescribable joy. His own words to me were nearly if not exactly these : " I first saw clearly the existence of God in walking along the bridge at Aberdeen; it was a great discovery to me ; I stopped and stood in an ecstasy of joy at seeing the existence of God." I think he also added, " I stood and thanked God for his existence." To another friend he gave the sequel of his admiring stance in its outburst of physical exultation : " When I was convinced that there was a God, I danced on the Brig o' Dee with delight."

To an onlooker his long years as a student seem to present a life of intolerable hardship, which only a will of iron could have passed through. Supporting himself by teaching, sometimes schools, sometimes individual pupils, having poor success either in teaching or in keeping his scholars, and a miserable pittance in return for his labours, he was often steeped in poverty, badly fed and uncomfortably clothed ; with no lively faith beyond the grave, and the hope distant, and uncertain, of at last reaching some living in the ministry. But he gained some present recompense in the intense delight which he always had in every mental exercise and acquisition. To be allowed to bury himself in books and thoughts, in philosophy, in languages, in literature, was far more enjoyment to him than to have received the largest emoluments that required his time and his talents for other objects. As regards the labour of teaching, that was no drudgery to him, except as any routine would have been, for he took a hearty delight in it to the end of his life. But with all his capacity for intellectual enjoyment, those dark and fruitless years were passed under a conscience not heavily burdened yet sensibly clouded, and always with a spirit unsatisfied and far from rest.

HIS CONVERSION.

O Sinner, Sinner, you have something in your power which no saint has. Repent, repent, and you will make all heaven ring for joy.—J.D.

His conversion I shall briefly relate as it presents itself to my recollection, as I have heard it at different times and in various portions. When Dr. Malan of Geneva visited Aberdeen in May 1826, Mr. Duncan had made very little progress in doctrinal faith, during the interval of eight years since the existence of God had broken fully on his mind; and in the midst of great intellectual and literary acquirements he had made no religious or moral advance. His creed was fruitless; " when he knew God, he glorified him not as God." With a theistic belief he was living without God in the world; and his whole condition, religious and moral, was very far from satisfying his own conscience. But he earnestly desired to see Malan. He often spoke to me with gratitude of the confidence he was prepared to put in him and of his readiness to receive his spiritual counsel; believing him to be thoroughly genuine, frank, and open. His intimate friend, Mr. David Brown, was from his own experience specially fitted to enter into his case, and on him was conferred the peculiar privilege of serving as one of the two earthly links in the chain of his conversion : no mean honour in the kingdom of heaven, and in itself no scanty fruit for a Christian life. In this crisis he was enabled to deal with him faithfully, tenderly, and wisely, and so pressed upon him the want of holiness as to leave him in a very softened state of mind.

It might be hard to find a broader contrast in two men of intellect than between César Malan and John Duncan : between the incessant questioning of the one, first on the authority, and next on the meaning of the Bible ; and the quick incisive way of the other, asking, " What is the use of a sword except to cut ? " and, without discussing the temper of the blade or the sharpness of its edge, using the Word of God directly, leaving no room to dispute its authority, and little to question its meaning. But the very contrast of the men fitted them for each other in the hands of God, when His hour had come. A man like Duncan himself would never have met his case : all dealing with him in his own way, however wisely and well, would have left him exactly where he was. Malan's method was one-sided, and far from suitable for every man. His great text was, " Whosoever believeth that Jesus is the Christ is born of God," and his constant question, " Do you believe that Jesus is the Christ ? " Some of those with whom he

conversed answered that they did believe that'
Jesus is the Christ, with satisfaction alike to
him and to themselves ; and accepted the conclusion of their own new birth, but with no
evidence of spiritual life preceding, accompanying, or following the confession. But he was a
man full of faith and zeal, and his word was
followed with power where cold statements of
truth were as lifeless as if they had been worth-
less ; and the prompt and high assurance which
he preached shook men out of that carnal and
fatal security, of which inalienable doubt is the
first and most essential element.

" Do you believe that Jesus is the Christ ? "
asked Malan of his scholar when they were
alone together, but he made no response. " Do
you believe that Jesus is the Christ ? " he
asked again, and was met with the same
silence. " Man, won't you speak ?—do you
believe that Jesus is the Christ ? " " But I
don't know what the Christ means." " Never
mind that just now,—do you believe that
Jesus is the Christ ? " " To tell you the truth,
I have been a Sabellian." " And I was a
Socinian,—let us leave that. Do you believe
that the Bible is the Word of God ? " " I believe that the Bible is the Word of God."
" You believe that the Bible is the Word of
God, and the Bible says that Jesus is the
Christ,—do you believe that Jesus is the
Christ ? " " But I don't know what the Christ
is." " Never mind that just now ; you believe
that the Bible is the Word of God, and the
Bible says that Jesus is the Christ,—do you

believe that Jesus is the Christ ? "   " I believe
that Jesus is the Christ." The Genevan pastor
carried through his reasoning, and went on :
" He that believeth that Jesus is the Christ is
born of God ;" and God, who is wonderful in
counsel and excellent in working, was even
then translating his child out of darkness into
his own marvellous light, and creating him
anew in Christ Jesus. As the conversation
proceeded, Duncan quoted a text of Scripture,
which Malan instantly seized :—" See, you
have got the Word of God in your mouth."
He replied in the words of the 119th Psalm,
—" And may He not take it utterly out of my
mouth." This reply, which he only once related to me, was not the least remarkable of
the words of that memorable hour. No other
man would have given such an answer ; and
never was a prayer more notably fulfilled, for
the Word of God did indeed remain in his
heart and in his mouth from that day onward
till the day of his death, as in no other man of
this age equally known to the Church. He
frequently spoke to me with deep impression
of that first direct communication from God to
his soul brought out in the thrilling announce-
ment : " The Word of God is in your mouth ;"
of the electric power which in that moment
accompanied the word that was at once in the
heart of God and in his own heart ; and of that
great beginning of all communion between God
and himself on earth and through eternity. Before leaving Aberdeen the quick-eyed foreigner,
hazarding a prediction which was illustriously

verified by the event, said to his friends : —
"That man will soon be before you all ; he
believes the Word of God."

The proud man had now been converted
into a little child, and he told us how he laid
himself down to rest night by night with the
infant's prayer in his lips :—

> " This night when I lie down to sleep,
> I give my soul to Christ to keep ;
> If I should die before I wake,
> I pray the Lord my soul to take."

More than forty years after, when near the end
of his course, a brother in the ministry finding
him in deep despondency tried to silence his
self-accusations and startle him out of his darkness by saying : "Now, Dr. Duncan, this is
all nonsense ; you know that when you go to
bed to-night you will commit yourself to God
in prayer, and you will not care much whether
you waken again in this world or not." The
old man was staggered and evidently comforted, and said : "It's quite true ; when I go
to bed I say the child's hymn :—

> ' This night when I lie down to sleep,
> I give my soul to Christ to keep.' "

He had been engaged to preach on the Sabbath following his conversion, but he felt his
recent knowledge too limited. "I had the
Gospel," he said to me, " but I had not Gospel
enough to mak' a sermon o'." In this strait he
put new wine into old bottles by interspersing
at the moment an old lifeless sermon with the
living words of salvation. But he soon broke
away from such trammels, and testified of

Christ with great power, preaching a high and instant assurance, and magnifying the glorious privileges of the Lord's people. In private he was full of zeal and love, and so pressed the great salvation on all that an old minister described him to me as "Like a policeman arresting people on the streets at night," and compelling them to come in.

A friendly controversy which he had with his landlady probably occurred about this time. She was a good woman, but a Wesleyan Methodist; he could not suffer her Arminianism, and she could not at all digest his Calvinism. The two had many a discussion, till at last, despairing of rectifying her theology, but admiring her grace, he closed their controversy with the judicial deliverance, "Madam, you are like your own clock : it strikes the wrong hour, but the hands are always right."

It was not to be looked for, that a mind so wide in its range as Dr. Duncan's would continue through life limited to the one cast of Scriptural teaching which he had learned in so brief a time, and to the one form of religious experience through which he had so quickly passed. Through a trust in Christ, which had very much the aspect of a simple acceptance of the testimony of God concerning his Son, John Duncan had been suddenly brought by the Spirit into light and liberty and holiness. He believed in the election of God, but consciously only after he had himself been called and justified ; he knew the necessity of being born again, but he learned that truth distinctly

after he had himself been begotten by the word
of truth ; he was taught to pray, but not as
one knocking outside the gate, but as having
already believed and entered into rest. All
this was of God ; it was the simplest, yet not
the only form of conversion.

That he should undergo a deeper teaching in
these and other great truths was a discipline
hardly to be avoided. " Hast thou found honey?
eat so much as is sufficient for thee,". was a
lesson he had yet to learn. But the leaving of
his first love, and the not holding fast but letting
go the truth, light, and liberty which he had
received, while graciously used for his teaching,
were certainly no essential elements in his
spiritual training. " Spiritual joy," he said
afterwards, " is a delicate thing, it requires
great tenderness ;" and he often said, " To the
hungry soul every bitter thing is sweet." The
rejoicing in Christ Jesus, of which he had tasted
largely, was the finest of the wheat ; but his
heart, though now become good ground, was
overcropped by a constant growing of the one
grain, and by forgetting the wisdom of the
husbandman, " who casts abroad the fitches,
and scatters the cummin, and casts in the
barley and the rye in their place." Through
want of watchfulness and self-scrutiny, of humi-
liation, repentance, tenderness, through a latent
antinomian tendency to adhere only to promise
and privilege and joy, through the magnifying of
faith and the practical disparagement of a good
conscience, the fruits of the Spirit withered,
the love, joy, peace, lost their beauty and

freshness. But the words were the same as before; the doctrinal assurance remained, but without the reality; and the profession of faith was as high as ever, while there lived no longer in its strength that faith which "endures as seeing Him who is invisible." The lips and the heart were not one. John Duncan could not long endure this hollowness; the Lord who had called him brought home to his conscience the warning, "First of all beware of the leaven of the Pharisees, which is hypocrisy;" the inflated air-vessel was pierced, and fell in with a terrible collapse. He fell into darkness, doubt, fear, all but absolute despair. He lost utterly all confidence in the past, had not one spark of light for the present, and only a ray of hope for the future. "You had a bright and true assurance of salvation after your conversion," I said to him, "how did you lose that assurance?" "Because I could keep it no longer without becoming a hypocrite; and whatever I am, I'm not a hypocrite, and won't be one." He saw that he was retaining the shadow without the substance, and he cast the shadow away that he might recover the substance.

He now also came under spiritual teachers with views widely different from the Genevese pastor's; men deeply taught by the Spirit, rich in grace, and highly honoured in their ministry; yet tending in their doctrine to keep God in Christ at an extreme distance, as Malan tried to force an extreme nearness. Merely to have substituted the second school of theology for the first had been a doubtful advantage ; and no doubt for a time the change partook of this character, and his teaching was too strongly marked by severity and distance. But throughout the long range of years afterwards, through by far the larger portion of his Christian life, Dr. Duncan held a marvellous fulness of the Word of God, and took it in its length and breadth as few men have ever done. Tens of thousands, from the dark bright hour in the jail of Philippi to the hour now passing, have been translated from darkness into light in the end as instantaneously and in the process almost as rapidly as John Duncan ; fewer, yet many, have undergone at conversion a discipline not equal, yet similar to his after his relapse ; but probably very few men indeed have passed through the two experiences with the same full entrance into both. Few have equally known the quickness, the simplicity, and the joy of his conversion, and the sorrow, the long darkness, and the deep pit out of which he was taken at his recovery.

After a conflict very protracted and tremendously severe, with a deep submission to the sovereign will of God, he was restored to a good measure of light and liberty. The conversion and the recovery in their combination present one of the most remarkable spiritual histories that have ever been recorded. As in everything else, so in these two experiences the extremes of spiritual exercise were combined ; and they formed the man in his long subsequent life. They mingled in all his

religion, moulded all his character, and leavened all his teaching. Each was the comple-
ment of the other; and if for a time the last
became first, the fervour and simplicity of the
first recovered and retained an equal place.
Through life his anger burned against a surface
Gospel; but it kindled as keenly at the Gospel
withheld or robbed of its simplicity.

His recovery he sometimes called his second
conversion, when he doubted the first. It was
similar to his view of a second baptism : which
came up in reference to persons who doubted
the validity of their infant baptism, because
their parents were ungodly, or because they
were Roman Catholics. He had no difficulty
about either case; but he would have administered baptism in both, if necessary for the ease
of troubled consciences. " I would use the
Church of England form : ' If thou art not
baptized, I baptize thee.' I like that form."
So if he was not truly converted the first time,
he trusted he was the second time. But he
always returned to the persuasion of the genu-
ineness of his original conversion; I doubt
if he ever let it quite go except in his first
great darkness; and he often spoke with the
highest assurance of the moment when the voice
of his God first broke in upon his soul. That
first entrance of the Word of God into his
heart he habitually regarded as the grand hour
in his existence, as the turning point between
life and death for time and eternity.

CHAPTER II.

PERSIE CHAPEL.

What is man's creation? *Being* like God.
What is the law ? Surely a very reasonable one : *Be* like God.—J. D.

In 1830 Mr. Duncan was appointed, but without ordination, to the very rural charge of Persie Chapel, in the eastern borders of Perthshire. On that brief period of pastoral duty he always looked back with the peculiar interest that usually clings to the first plot of ground allotted to a minister in his Master's vineyard ; and when his preaching was complained of as too deep for Glasgow and Edinburgh, he used to defend himself by the intelligence of his country people at Persie, who could comprehend any theology spoken in Saxon, although it was too hard for the citizen intellect. While theological terms to define the nicest shades of meaning were quite familiar to him, he had a singular power of expressing the deepest theological truths with the most exact precision in the simplest and commonest words. Some notes of this period, partly by one of our respected ministers, and partly from one of Dr. Duncan's own relatives, will help to show the turn of his thoughts and the character of his early ministry.

29

" Mr. Duncan had heard of a student being in his neighbourhood, and he came to my father's to seek me out. After returning from a long solitary walk, I was told that the new Persie minister had been inquiring for me, and that, after sitting for some time in the house, he had gone out, and was somewhere about in the fields. After some search I found him sound asleep upon a broken coil of hay, with a strong autumn sun beating on his face.

" He was easily persuaded to remain over the night ; and although, after a lapse of more than forty years few reminiscences of the conversation remain with me, yet I have a vivid recollection of the fascinating influence which he exerted over me ; and while I remained in the country I was during that season pretty frequently with him. We were looking at the opening verses of the Gospel of John, and pausing at the latter clause of verse 3, he asked me what I understood by the expression, καὶ χωρὶς αὐτοῦ ἐγένετο οὐδὲ ἓν, ὃ γέγονεν. I said that I supposed it to be just a re-assertion, in a stronger form, of the statement in the preceding clause. ' No, no,' was the reply ; ' it is far more than that. The Spirit of God is not guilty of tautology. The Evangelist means to close the mouth of the Arian. " All things were made by him," *all things that ever were made,* for " without him was there not anything made that was made ;" so that He Himself *cannot* be a creature.' " [6]

SABBATH-BREAKING.

An Elijah-like zeal and faithfulness, mingled with love, seems to have been the prevailing characters stamped on this period of his ministry, as will appear in the following incident :—
" More than once I heard him preach in the parish church of Kirkmichael, during that, or the early part of the following season; and I can, at this distance of time, recall the very words of a passage in one of his closing prayers. It was in allusion to the practice of holding Privy Council Meetings on the Sabbath-day. ' O Lord, bless our sinful, godless, Sabbath-breaking Privy Council. Thou knowest that Thou art not honoured there, for they profane Thy holy day by their meetings for State business. O Lord,' he went on, ' bless the high courts of Parliament now assembled. Thou knowest that Thou art not honoured there ; where potsherd warreth with potsherd. Do Thou be there to overrule their deliberations.'

" I forget if it was on the same day that an incident occurred, furnishing as striking an exemplification of moral power as anything that I ever saw or read of. From time immemorial it had been the practice, in the parish of Kirkmichael, for the church-officer to ' cry the roups,' as it was called, *i.e.* to proclaim on the Sabbath-day, after the dismissal of the congregation, all the public roups that were to take place in the parish during the current week. Efforts had been frequently made, by influential parties in the parish, to put an end to this unseemly practice, but without success. Mr. Duncan had closed the service, and was walking up the steep road towards the manse, leaning heavily on my arm, for he was much exhausted. The congregation, having left the church, were standing part in the graveyard, and part above upon the public road, which looked down over a sunk fence upon the churchyard. In the midst of this latter group stood the church-officer, who proceeded to cry his roups.

"The moment Mr. Duncan heard his voice, he exclaimed, 'There's the devil begun the moment I have closed my mouth.' 'Let us go on,' I said; 'the practice is inveterate; we have done all we could to stop it, but without effect.' 'I believe,' he replied, 'you are right.' We walked on a few steps to the manse door. Evidently the fire within was burning fiercely. At last he flung away my arm and cried, 'I'll not stand that; you may go or stay as you like.' We rapidly retraced our steps. The people opened up a lane for us, to come up side by side with the beadle. He made a pause, when Mr. Duncan immediately struck in with, 'Is the devil over with his roups? If he is, then I, a servant of the Lord Jesus, will intimate a roup also: "Remember the Sabbath to keep it holy."' In tones of awful solemnity he repeated the words of the commandment, and then added: 'My friends, there's the roup of a holy Sabbath to you. Sanctify it to God or to the devil as you please. I have done my duty!' Not another word was spoken. I was told that the poor beadle went off the ground uttering curses, not loud but deep ; but not another roup was from that day cried in the parish." [6]

DANCING.

The same burning zeal is brought out in some other incidents, arising out of different occasions, but otherwise not unlike in character to the last. Either during his work at Persie, or in the earlier part of his ministry in Glasgow, he went on a visit to Aberdeen, and was invited with some of his mother's kinsfolk to a marriage at a farm somewhere in the neighbourhood. After the ceremony the party adjourned to the barn for a dance. Mr. Duncan did not join them, but remained alone in the house, for he strongly disapproved of dancing, as tending to a relaxation of morality ; but "there's no sin," he said, "in saltatory motion, and there can be no harm in brothers and sisters dancing together." His friends were not content either with his absence from the company, or with his owl-like occupancy of the farmhouse by himself in the loneliness of the night ; their inhospitality, his unhappiness, and the condemnation of their revelry were all involved in his seclusion. Although he told them that he disapproved of dancing, they would have him join their party in the barn, but he steadfastly refused ; they pressed him further, and he replied,—"If I am present, I must stop you ; but if you let me stay here, you may go on with your dancing. I'll not interfere with you." But the compromise failed to satisfy their conscience and their kindness; he was the last man to grace their festivity, but they would not dance on without him; they did not see how his presence could arrest their gaiety, and they urged him till he consented. On entering he sat down quietly among them till they danced out their reel, with a pleasure less mingled now that they had got happily filled the only void in the barn. But as soon as the dance was ended he rose up, and planting his back against the door to prevent escape, he turned the gay ball into a grave and astonished audience, listening to a severe sermon on the evils attaching to promiscuous dancing. After the address was finished he admonished several of his friends individually. One of them justified herself with the triumphant reply, "I've not been dancing;" but in handing her into her gig on leaving the house he surprised her with the sharpness of his remark,—"Ah, cousin, I see now how you did not dance; no thanks to people not committing sin when they're not able." His worthy cousin was lame from having sprained her ankle.

IDLE WORDS.

During his residence at Persie, or about that time, a gentleman having a distinguished minister in his house on a visit, invited a large party of ministers and others to meet him at dinner, and Mr. Duncan was among the guests.

The benevolent lady presiding at the table, who abounded in good works, had also an abundant stream of words, and in her remarks threw in the frequent preface, "Upon my honour." The expletive had offended Mr. Duncan several times during dinner, till at last he could tolerate it no longer, and looking across the table he asked, "What is your honour worth, madam?" The rough question startled the company, and silenced the astonished tongue for a time; but the lady generously acknowledged afterwards that her censor was right, and, if we mistake not, the expression was disused by her in after life.[6]

These incidents regarding this period happen to be of one character, marked by a holy severity, but his ministry at Persie was not the less on that account full of tenderness and love. He was attached to the people and they were attached to him with a truly mutual affection. A good many years after he had left them he preached in a neighbouring parish, where a large and interested congregation of his old friends gathered to hear him. Touched with the sight, and with the evidence it gave of their remembrance and affection, he said to them, "I know you love me, but I did not die for you."

CHAPTER III.

MINISTRY IN GLASGOW.

Every fibre of my soul winds itself round that ("Enjoyment of
God for ever") with unutterable, sickening, fainting desire.
Oh that the Beloved may be mine, and I His, and I His,
and I His.—J. D.

IN the summer of 1831 Mr. Duncan was
called from Persie to Glasgow to take an afternoon lectureship in Duke Street Gaelic Chapel;
he gave also a week-evening lecture, an addi-
tion to myself most memorable.

HIS PREACHING.

In the end of that year, during the Christ-
mas recess of the Edinburgh Divinity Hall,
I was asked to accompany a friend to his
church ; and the first time that I saw him was
in hearing him preach to his small evening
congregation, dotted sparsely over the large
building. It was one of those grand bursts of
heavenly eloquence, in which the whole man
seemed to soar into an upper region in which
I never remember to have seen any one but
himself; certainly no other on quite the same
height, and himself but rarely there. As was
well said of him on another occasion, " The

man was at his best, and *a wonderful best it was.*" It was not the intellect taking a lofty flight while the spirit was weak; or the strength of the spirit bearing up the feebler intellect; but his flight was poised equally on both pinions, and the body itself seemed ready to be borne upward. The spirit had pierced the clouds, and the mind brought down the spiritual conceptions and unveiled them in their own beauty. His reading of the Scriptures, which was at all times quite singular in expressiveness, was then radiant with heavenly light.

He was in a course of lectures on the Trinity; he had discoursed on the Person and the glory of the Father, and on the Son as the eternally begotten of the Father; and he was that evening to have gone on to the consideration of the Holy Ghost as proceeding from the Father and the Son. "This ought to have been our subject to-night," he said, "but it is too much, and we must pause. The human mind is incapable of searching long into these high mysteries; if without special grace an angel were to continue gazing on them, he would be transformed into a devil before he ended. Let us therefore turn aside for a little from looking on the lightning glare, and let us contemplate some of the objects which may be seen by its reflection. Let us consider, not God, but man made after the image of God; not a little being, as many think him, but great and noble. Men seek to cast contempt on God by spoiling the work of his hands; they make themselves

vile, and reproach their Maker as if he had
created them mean. Man is a ruin, but he is
a noble ruin."   On this subject he said, a year
before his death, "The Jews referred the 8th
Psalm to Adam, but it refers to Christ the
second Adam. This circumstance is both its
veil and its beauty. There is a comparison
and a contrast; it takes man as fallen, but
speaks of him as still great, so that he must be
restored to his condition. The only solution
of sin and misery compatible with God's be-
nignity and holiness is the fall." [13]   He said
again,—"Sin is a monstrous, unnatural, miserable thing. We should remember we were in
Adam standing before we were in Adam fallen;
creation was before the fall. Man is of noble
descent, though he has become of ignoble character. Men should be living like dethroned
princes; that is but half the truth; believers
should be living like restored princes. Back
to the Adamic likeness to God we cannot come,
this is done for ever; believers are not pre-
destinated to be conformed to the image of the
unfallen Adam, but to the image of Christ.
Oh what a solemn thing it is to be a man!
made so exalted, fallen so low, capable of being
raised again so high."

On such occasions his language was concise,
oracular, and singularly beautiful; every word
was a thought, sought out as a jewel, and fitted
artistically in its place. His discourse was not
one idea presented in many forms, nor many
ideas filled up with looser materials, nor a
chain of successive arguments; but a unity

made up of parts, each fine in itself, and each helpful to the whole, fitted together as in a beautiful mosaic, and lighted up with the frequent flashes of sanctified genius. In beauty it was a picture; but in power it was the rushing of sparkling wine that had burst its bottles.

At some other times, however, his preaching was the slow utterance of thoughts that seemed to be gathering themselves in drops when he was in the pulpit; big drops, but with great intervals between them; and the whole occupying an excessive time before he could be satisfied that there was enough in the cup to offer to the soul of the weary. Latterly his preaching was more equal; occasionally but not often as lofty, and seldom on the other hand so diffuse.

"His preaching," writes a friend, "was too abstract for most men. He had lived among abstractions till they had come to exercise over him the power of concrete realities. Moral ideas—holiness, justice, goodness and truth— waked strongest emotion in him. For him they were never mere notions, but always divine properties. The personality of God energized them. Though in his discourses he used very abstract language, he realized and made others feel that he was speaking not of theological notions, but of the personal Jehovah. His fervid devotional feeling uttered itself not in sensuous imagery, but in lofty abstractions. It had in it more of the sublime than the tender." [12]

His exposition of Scripture, when he did

not allow himself to linger over a single verse, but took a psalm or a passage of some length, was eminently of the very highest character, and in its kind quite unequalled by any exposition to be heard elsewhere. It neither filled up the text with a meaning not its own, nor drained it all but dry to meet the emptiness of the interpreter's own mind; but brought out what was in the words, at once so clearly and so richly, that the hearer, while ashamed of his own dulness in not seeing it before, rejoiced in the opened abundance of grace and truth.

His devotional exercises that first evening were not less striking than his sermon. His prayers were more than any other man's marked by a sense of the majesty of the holy Lord God, and a perception of the Divine glory, especially in the earlier part of his course. In his latter years Christ was more the centre of all his thoughts, as seems to be often the case with eminent saints; Rutherford's wondrous letters have almost nothing of the Father or of the great God, except as seen in Jesus Christ. In the earlier period of Dr. Duncan's course, his view of the Divine glory was often the same as Isaiah's, "Woe is me, because I am a man of unclean lips, for mine eyes have seen the King, the Lord of hosts;" and as Job's, "I have heard of thee by the hearing of the ear, but now mine eye seeth thee, wherefore I abhor myself." Latterly this holy fear was modified, but it continued to the end; and the enviable epitaph found on some of our old gravestones might most fittingly have been written on his, " Deceased in the fear of God."

He sometimes said, " I incline to think that prayer should be all in the words of Scripture ;" and his own prayers, by no means always but frequently, were expressed very much in Bible language. They were often such as to humble in the dust every one that joined in the worship : " The King scattering iniquity with his eyes ; the Lord great in Zion ; let us praise thy great and terrible name, for it is holy ; thou lovest judgment, thou establishest equity ; honour and majesty are before Thee, strength and beauty are in thy sanctuary ; how great is thy goodness, how great is thy beauty !" Such words, if there was little strength in his own spirit at the time, might have little effect on others. But when he was full of the Holy Ghost and of power, it was the language of one standing within the veil, describing what he saw himself at the moment, and compelling others to feel that they stood on holy ground, with their feet within the gate of heaven.

" Pray for me," was perhaps of all expressions the most frequent on his lips ; his friends seldom met him without having this burden laid upon them. In one of his fits of depression he made this request to a young friend whom he met in walking, and was answered by an expression of unfitness to pray for *him*. But he followed up his plea by asking : " In whose name do you pray? not in your own ;" and got so interested in talking of the ground of acceptance in prayer being the merits of Christ alone that for a time he seemed to throw off the load. He complained, " When I make known my case to my friends they are more inclined to preach to me than to pray for me. 'Is there no balm in Gilead? Is there no physician there?' But we shall not heal ourselves by merely applying the labels in the apothecary's shop, and that is the most we can do for one another. The balm in Gilead must be applied by the Physician there."

DREAD OF A SHALLOW RELIGION.

The first time I called on him in Glasgow, about the year 1832, he was in a state of self-jealousy from a sense of spiritual distance and coldness. The cause was peculiar, as assigned by himself. He said, " It is a trying time for a man when he has been seven years converted. At first he is often in the 142d Psalm ; ' refuge fails him,' and that keeps him near; after that he has a great many difficulties to solve, which keep him praying; but at the end of seven years he is out of his first straits, and he has got most of his questions answered ; he stops inquiring, and is apt to settle on his lees and get into darkness."

Three or four years later, in 1836, he brings out vividly in a letter from Glasgow one of his leading and life-long jealousies, his fear of a shallow religion. He feared this first and most for himself, and then he feared it for the religious community, with a singularly sensitive apprehension. The " gentle conviction of sin, the calm, coldish admiration of Christ, the gentlemanly, scholarlike, prudent gratitude, the obedience of a freezing but not absolutely frozen state," he detected in others as well as dreaded in himself; and there was nothing into which he more earnestly entered, than any preaching or line of procedure that would help to break up such a condition of the Christian church. At all costs he would have it broken up in himself; and he did not care what offence of the cross might arise, what foolishness of preaching, what contempt of the worldly world, or what displeasure of the religious world might ensue, if there might by any means be a shaking of this stagnation in the Christian community. The following sentences contain one of the deepest and most abiding of all his thoughts, or habits of thought, from the period of his conversion and recovery to the day of his death. Apart from these views Dr. Duncan's religion can never be rightly understood, and their apprehension is the key to one-half of his religious thoughts concerning both himself and others.

" Your complaint of the hardness of your heart touched a sore in myself, which I was rather desirous to have left alone. I was desirous of maintaining a quiet, gentle conviction of sin, which could comport with a distant regard to Christ's salvation ; a faint hope, a calm, coldish admiration, a gentlemanly, scholarlike, theologian-like, prudent, *very prudent* gratitude ; and as much obedience as would result from such a freezing, I hope not absolutely frozen, state of affections. My chastisement, I think, I may say I hope (awful hope !), has begun. Week before last a terrible dread of everlasting misery seized me. Nor that alone; I *do* think (would that I were sure) that the thought of being without God *in the world* is abhorrent to my heart. I cannot exercise it well, it is so dark, fickle, tumultuous. But oh, it doth deceive me much if there be not there some deep-seated, though overlaid and crushed down, yet true desire for union to the Lord Jesus Christ; something that would if it could cry, 'Oh that the God and Father of our Lord Jesus Christ would strengthen with all might *by his Spirit* in the inner man, that Christ may dwell in the heart by faith.'"

INTENSE LOVE TO GOD.

A most vivid contrast to the "distant regard, coldish admiration, and prudent gratitude," is exhibited in another letter of the same year. Seldom perhaps, except in the burning thirst of David's soul, has the whole heart of a man been so attracted to God. Language can hardly embody a stronger utterance of desire than in the words :—"Every fibre of my soul winds itself round the enjoyment of God for ever with unutterable, sickening, fainting desire;" and every one who knew the writer can attest his transparent sincerity, and the clear evidence of the strength of his thoughts exceeding the force of his words. To have possessed a man so intensely devoted to God is a blessing and an honour to his generation and to his land.

"To whom shall we go but unto Thee? Thou hast the words of *eternal life.* I would wish to be in such a frame of mind as to put the chief emphasis on ' *Thou ;*' but while I do feel deeply interested about religion, the Christian religion, Jehovah and his religion, selfishness is the presently predominating element. I desire my own happiness; I know and feel that God in Christ alone can constitute that happiness; but in answering the question, ' What is man's chief end ?' I pass over the first part mainly with an intellectual approbation of its moral rectitude as a requirement, ' Man's chief end is to glorify God;' while every fibre of my soul winds itself round the latter part ('to enjoy Him for ever') with unutterable, sickening, fainting desire. But I pray the Lord my God to circumcise my heart to love the Lord my God, to love Him for his own essential, revealed excellencies with *devoted* love; that the Beloved (O my soul, O Spirit of the Lord, is He or is He not *my* Beloved?) may be mine, and I his, and I his, *and I his.*"

DR. JOHN MUIR.

By the liberality of his friends a new church was built for him, called Milton Church, and in it he was ordained to the ministry in 1836. A year or two after, Dr. Muir of Glasgow and Dr. Duncan happened on one occasion to be colleagues in preaching for me at a communion season, and they fell into a theological discussion, chiefly on the term Θεοτόκος, Mother of God, applied to the Virgin Mary. The two minds were both acute, but excepting divine grace, and love for each other as servants of one Lord, they had little in common. Dr. Duncan had great reverence for the ancient Church. He used to say, " Let us speak tenderly of the faults of the Old Testament saints ; " and a book, consisting of extracts of erroneous passages from the writings of the Fathers, he denounced with great vehemence, saying, " It is a Ham-like book ! " But quite apart from its antiquity, he zealously defended the term in question, because the Virgin Mary was the Mother of Him who is God, and who never was not God. Dr. Muir revered the Bible, but no authority besides, and he must have everything direct and clear, with no mystery about it. The argument continued for perhaps the greater part of two hours. The disputants got further removed from each other as it advanced, and it ended with considerable warmth on both sides. Dr. Muir denounced the term as Popish blasphemy, and before leaving his patience was nearly exhausted toward its defender. When he had left, his friend remarked,—" That man owes much to divine grace ; except for grace Dr. Muir would have been a Socinian." Some one having remarked that his sermon was good, he replied,—" There was a great deal of good English in that discourse ; " while after another address he said,—" How forcible are right words ! "

ROBERT M'CHEYNE.

" M'Cheyne's mind plays about the lighter aspects of theology," was an old criticism of Dr. Duncan's, which I have had great hesitation in writing down, both because the estimate is not just in itself, and because he would probably have withdrawn it in his riper age, for he survived M'Cheyne twenty-seven years. M'Cheyne's doctrine was not so profound as his own; but with all his gentleness he exceeded Dr. Duncan in a holy severity, and even sternness, and in his teaching he was far from shunning the severer aspects of divine truth. But I have written Dr. Duncan's words because it may help to bring out some parts of his character more distinctly, if we compare them with corresponding, or rather with contrasted features in the character of Mr. M'Cheyne.

M'Cheyne and he both used to assist me at Communions; they met each other, and heard each other preach; they loved and honoured each other in the Lord; but their minds were in many respects unlike, and were not mutually attractive. The genius in Duncan and the poetry in M'Cheyne were indeed of one family; but these lines of kindred were lost in a general unlikeness, and I question if M'Cheyne learned almost anything from Dr. Duncan, who was neither lucid enough nor joyful enough for him. He had not the opportunity, like William Burns, of sitting under his ministry; but if he had been in Glasgow he would probably have preferred Dr. John Muir, whose lively exposition of the gospel he enjoyed, and of whom he used to say, " Muir is imputed righteousness to the backbone." M'Cheyne with all his meekness had a resolute will; his views of divine truth were clear and determined before he knew Dr. Duncan, and were of a simpler character; and he did not readily yield his matured thoughts to be moulded even by men of the highest intellect.

M'Cheyne's strength was in his rare singleness of eye, which kept the whole body full of light, and in which it was hard to name his equal. Duncan with all his abstraction was not always free from self-consciousness; and would occasionally make or repeat his remarks, not from the simple impulse of the moment, and with a mingling of self-satisfaction. The elements of M'Cheyne's mind and character were admirably mingled. In his doctrine, in his experience, in his daily walk, he was so free from extremes, that want of variety and tameness might have been anticipated as the result; but on the contrary the Lord had moulded him to fit as great a multitude of minds as if his thoughts had been commonplace, while they were full of strength and beauty. In Duncan, thoughts, experience, and all things about him, not mingled and tempered at all, poured out in large separate masses with which few minds found sympathy. Many of M'Cheyne's hearers would have thought that the effect of his preaching was partly owing to a halo of interest attaching to himself, and that his words would lose not a little when committed to print; but they are more powerful when read and when dissevered from all that was adventitious. Duncan was far more dependent on an audience, although a very small one would satisfy him; and his thoughts did not lose but gained immensely by its presence. If it could not be termed his oratory, it was his spirit, his voice, his manner, and his nice balancing of the power of all his words; so that if they had been written down word for word, some of his ideas would seem to have been lost in the transference, and the whole to have been not a little impoverished.

M‘Cheyne, whose writings since his death have been so largely read and with so much profit, was himself disposed in the later years of his brief career to read little except the Bible. Duncan, who wrote nothing for others to read, was an omnivorous reader of other men's writings. M‘Cheyne was scrupulously methodical; Duncan entirely devoid of method. M‘Cheyne with all his poetry did not care for what was speculative, but liked all that was practical; practical in theology, practical in spiritual exercise, practical in dealing with the conscience, practical in duty. In conversing on our relation to Christ, he said to me in his practical way, " I hold Christ's work to be mainly a plan of recovery." " Yes; but through eternity these words will continue true, ' I am the vine, and ye are the branches.' " " When you put it in that way," he replied, " I cannot answer you." But when I made some other statement, the solidity of which he questioned, he closed my lips by asking, " Would you

preach that to your people ?" These practical
habits of mind were the exact antipodes of Dr.
Duncan's ; and to know him the picture has
only to be reversed. Yet he could speak well
on a practical subject, and would say admirably, " Christ does not ask, ' What think ye
more than others ?' but ' What do ye more
than others ?' " The one, while no stranger to
sorrow, walked in a clear and quiet daylight ;
the other soared to the home of the lightning
and the secret place of thunder, and was apt to
sink again into the darkness of chaos. If an
intimate friend of both may venture to judge,
Duncan had more to contend with in himself,
was less watchful, less equal, and less helpful to
others in daily intercourse ; but had a deeper
conviction of sin, higher views of the glory of
God, fuller discoveries of Christ, a more inward
entrance into the secret of his pavilion, and a
holiness more intensely desired, but more inter-
mittingly held.

WILLIAM BURNS.

While Dr. Duncan's direct influence in conversion was limited, few men took so deep an
interest in the work of conversion through
others, and he was remarkably used and honoured in that relation. William Burns, who
was more employed in such work than any
other preacher in Scotland, owed to him under
God those deep views of divine truth which so
fitted him for the evangelistic field, and so
moved him to enter into it. With his con-

version he had nothing to do, but he was the
main instrument in his more special preparation for reaping that great Gospel harvest. " I
was not his spiritual father," he said, " but I
think I was his nurse." It always appeared to
me that except for Dr. Duncan's spiritual influence and teaching, William Burns would
never have been the great evangelist he was.
Their two minds seemed, indeed, to have
nothing in common except a singular aptitude
for languages in both ; and even in this they
were very different, because Burns's practical
turn came out in a fluent use of living tongues,
in which the other was quite defective. Before
he went to China, Dr. Duncan, who urged and
prevailed with him to go, said,—" You need not
expect ever to acquire Chinese so as to speak
it ; you must be satisfied with writing it." Yet
in a few years he learned not only to speak the
Chinese, but to interpret between Chinamen of
different provinces.

While he studied in Glasgow, some years after
his conversion, and when the edge of his spirit
had been partially blunted, he received under
Dr. Duncan's ministry a new and far deeper
baptism of the Spirit than at first, by which he
was specially fitted for the work to which he
was to be called. At a large meeting of those
who had profited by his ministrations in Perth,
he said,—" If you have got any good from me,
you owe it all to that remarkable man of God,
Dr. Duncan of Edinburgh. I have just taught
you what he has taught me." He added,
" When leaving Edinburgh, I asked him, ' What

advice will you now give me?' He answered,
'Take you care of his cause, and he will take
care of your interests; look after his glory,
and he will look after your comfort.'" [2]

Dr. Duncan's deep views of Divine realities
came out in a practical form in the ministry of
William Burns, who was endowed with a strong
will, an indomitable energy, an unflinching
courage, and an unfailing self-possession and
practical shrewdness, which were all of them
lacking in his spiritual father.

Perhaps the one spiritual feature that was
exactly and conspicuously the same in both
was their deep sense of " the exceeding sinfulness of sin;" but the spiritual affinity was
very marked in most of their leading characteristics, although modified by their mutual
differences.   The greatness of God, and the
value of his own soul in Dr. Duncan, came out
in Burns's practical mind in the greatness of
eternity and the value of the souls of many;
but each of these elements was strong in both.

Burns did not question his own conversion
like Duncan, but he was quite as sensible of
spiritual desertion and darkness, and at some
periods of his ministry was quite as frequent
with the cry :—" O wretched man that I am!
who shall deliver me from the body of this
death ?"   When a good Wesleyan minister
said to him in one of these states,—" We
should let our light shine before men," he
quietly replied,—" But what if there's no
light to shine ?"   This was just Dr. Duncan's
spiritual exercise in a slightly modified form.

On the other hand Dr. Duncan, though so anxiously occupied with the state of his own soul, was singularly alive to every awakening in the souls of others. When in 1839 there was that great awakening which spread over much of the country, he had no influence at the moment on the beginning of William Burns's revival power, which he received neither from man, nor by man, but from God by the Spirit. Burns was not living in Glasgow at the time ; but while ministering to Mr. M'Cheyne's church at Dundee, he visited his father at Kilsyth, and in preaching after the communion the Spirit came with great power on himself and on his hearers. But Dr. Duncan was one of the first to visit the scene, for his heart was absorbed in the work as soon as it commenced. So it was always to the close of his life ; he was sensitively alive to every work of the Spirit in the conversion of men to God, and no other interest could turn him aside from entering into such a work with all his heart, as the greatest and most attractive of all interests. However engrossed with other objects, any spiritual awakening near him would immediately engage his whole heart and mind. At Kilsyth he preached with great power from the words,—" Deliver from going down to the pit : I have found a ransom." He also conversed earnestly with Mr. Burns on bringing out more broadly the sovereignty of God in his preaching, and said to him,—" To leave out election is to leave out the keystone of the arch." In his later years he held the same truth

quite as firmly, but did not insist on its having
so large a place in the preaching of the Gospel
as during his ministry in Glasgow. If it was
not denied or set aside, he listened with delight and approval to preaching in which it
found less place than at Kilsyth.

Next to William Burns, there was perhaps
scarcely any man in our church who surpassed
Dr. Duncan in a deep, abiding, life-long interest
in the reviving of the work of God in the
land ; and he entered into it with a fulness of
sympathy peculiar to himself. He joined in
sympathy with those who waited in prayer
for the outpouring of the Spirit, he took part
with God's children in praising the Lord for
his goodness, and he dealt individually with
inquirers.   He was in sympathy with the
preachers in yearning with pity for perishing
men, and in testifying repentance toward God
and faith toward the Lord Jesus Christ, and
he loved to take part in their preaching.   But
he was also in sympathy with the awakened
hearers in the personal exercise of repentance
and faith, and in " desiring as a new-born babe
the sincere milk of the word," and sometimes
he seated himself among the inquirers as one
of them.   He did so afterwards within two
years of his death ; and he did so at this
time on one occasion at Kilsyth, when Mr.
Burns had invited inquirers to remain and to
take seats set apart for themselves.   Some of
the assisting ministers were not prepared for
this step, and did not enter into it; but to
their astonishment Dr. Duncan went forward

to one of the separated seats. His friends, supposing that he had made a mistake, went up to him and said,—" That seat is for the anxious." " But I 'm anxious," was his earnest reply. He did not take his place as one out of Christ, but as anxious to know if he was certainly in Christ.

So extreme a step was occasioned by his extreme doubting of his own salvation ; yet doubt was not the only nor perhaps the chief ingredient. The only elements he had no sympathy with were pride, hardness of heart, ungodliness, worldliness. Of an orthodox minister he would sometimes say, " He 's too unbroken for me ;" but wherever there was spiritual work he would enter into it in all its spheres. For him to seat himself among the inquirers was not going outside the spiritual circle, but was numbering himself with those who were repenting toward God and seeking the Lord Jesus Christ. It arose from a mistaken view of his own relation to God ; but his state of mind was not what a stranger would have inferred from his inquiring attitude, which was really not very far from the place of the saint rejoicing in Christ, and of the preacher witnessing to His grace. To him the whole lay within the circle of those whom the Spirit was teaching and leading.

His doubt was a great and evident defect ; yet, while the praise cannot be assigned to the doubt, there were spiritual fruits accompanying it which are comparatively rare, and which seem to be often hindered by assurance per-

verted into self-confidence. During forty-five
years of a pilgrim life in the wilderness, he
preserved his heart in a singular childlike softness, and his conscience most sensitively tender.
To a degree far higher than in most believers,
he was "kept by the power of God" from all
hardness of heart, and throughout his course
he "took heed to himself, lest he should be
hardened by the deceitfulness of sin." From
first to last he listened with an open ear to
the words, "To-day, if ye will hear his voice,
harden not your hearts."

In the awakening in Ireland in 1859, and
that which followed in Scotland, he took the
same interest as in Kilsyth twenty years before. At one season of this latter period of
spiritual concern, judging partly from what he
saw, and partly from the impression on his
own spirit, he said,—"We are within a very
little of a general awakening among the working classes in Edinburgh ;" but the tide receded
before reaching its fulness. He thoroughly
understood the manifold sifting to which such
a work must be subjected in the end ; but he
was not staggered in rejoicing over the fair blossoms and promises of fruit, although he knew
well that much that promised fair would bring
forth no fruit to perfection. Regarding the
signs of a saving change he exercised a large
catholicity of judgment. There was no kind
of spiritual exercise to which he was himself
a stranger, from the highest to the lowest,
from the deepest to the simplest, and he rejoiced in every varied token of spiritual life.

But he had himself, after his acceptance of Christ, learned much experimentally in the conviction of sin, in acquiescence in the Divine sovereignty, and in other spiritual teachings which many are taught before obtaining any sense of forgiveness ; and when he was asked regarding any particular element of spiritual light being essential to conversion, his answer was, " It is one of the teachings of the Spirit, but a man does not need to learn it before his conversion. If he is a child of God he will be taught it some time, either before or after, sooner or later."

HIS MARRIAGE.

" I have all my life been very dependent on women, and much indebted to female society," was one of his own sayings which all his friends could confirm. He had many thoughts about the relation of the sexes, which I now regret that I did not think of writing, and which unwisely I did not allow him to open up for want of time, when he was one day full of the subject ; but it was one of his many subjects of careful scrutiny.

" The most immoral song," he said, " I have ever heard, is one called 'Love not.' I have never heard it without loathing, nor, I may say, without reproving. Offensive songs I have heard, but none so immoral, cutting at the root of all morality. You are not to love the things, because they are changing, because they are perishing. Well, if they be so, let

them be loved with a love corresponding to
that ; but every creature of God is good, and
is to be loved."

In this connexion another thought may be
noticed, which came up in many forms through
all his meditations. " We must always remember," he said, " that man was created
before he fell. It is good to take a walk in
Eden." Of the kindness of God toward fallen
man he often spoke as the " philanthropy of
God," quoting Titus iii. 4 ; and while he took
a deep interest in everything truly philanthropic, he said,—" We cannot be more philanthropic than the philanthropic Jehovah."[9] "Let
us not," he said again, "neglect the body ; it
was created before the soul, and it was assumed
by Christ." Sometimes he felt the fall of man
so deeply, that he might have expected to
think of little else regarding him ; but few
men thought more strongly of sin as not a creature but the negation of good, or spoke more
frequently of God as the good Creator of good.
" God made man good, but it was a good that
was capable of a betterness ; it was not good
for man to be alone."—"Female beauty is set
forth in an architectural image : God *built* the
woman." [5] (Gen. ii. 22.)

The manner of his " indebtedness to female
society " was perhaps the last element in his
history, which any man conversant with his
character and ways would have filled up by
any conjecture at all resembling the facts.
That a man so innocent of practical shrewdness and common sense, and so easily imposed

upon at all hands, so ready to think well of everybody except himself, should have four times made an admirable choice of a lady for the head of his house, twice as a wife and twice as a companion, can only be attributed to God's very special care and guiding ; yet indicating also on his part a great power of discerning character when he was deeply interested. On the other hand, that the absent, untidy, discourteous, outré, and irreclaimably irregular and unconformable John Duncan should have succeeded in attracting to himself successively four ladies of refinement and of marked superiority among their sex, must likewise be regarded as a token of the Lord's goodness ; and at the same time as implying on his part a natural attractiveness which a superficial observer would not have suspected. The superiority of his intimate female friends may also be attributed to the fact that none but superior women would have cared for him, or could have endured him ; especially at the period of his first marriage in 1837, to Miss Janet Tower of Aberdeen, at a time when he had been untried in such a relation, and when his habits had not been modified by its salutary influence, while she had been accustomed to every refinement. " I believe Miss Tower is a superior woman," I remarked to a lady in Glasgow. " Of course," she replied, " none but a most superior woman would ever marry John Duncan."

The first great attraction in her case, as in all the others, was his deep piety ; next to

that, we are apt to suppose, came his great
mental powers ; and afterwards probably that
great personal attractiveness which was less
obvious on the surface. But John Duncan
was a truly loveable man, for grace, for genius,
for amiableness, for affection, for true refinement, for magnanimity, for companionableness,
for deep and lasting friendship. At the time
of the engagement, Miss Tower felt how critical
her position was in writing to him, because
she knew that her letters would lie open to all
the inmates or visitors of his lodgings, and she
charged him to burn her first letter after reading it. He replied, " Your request I have
ventured to disobey, till I receive a second
command. The epistle has been not for a
moment out of my personal custody, and I
have ordered a neat tin receptacle (with a
padlock attached, the key of which I can
always carry about with me), in which, if
permitted, letters would be inserted, as its sole
use. I am absent and careless, but this is a
matter too near my heart to be affected by the
same habits which affect other things."

These letters were always carefully kept
by themselves, in the hopeless confusion of
all things else, and still remain as they were
written. To have enjoyed his letters in return
demanded deep piety on her part for entering
into the religious feeling with which they are
filled, with an accomplished mind and a measure
of linguistic ardour to appreciate their other
contents. He sets himself to teach her Greek,
covers his paper with Greek inflexions in bold

characters, illustrates this by a comparison with
the structure of Latin, crosses his writing, and
fills with compact sentences every available
quarter of an inch of space in the margins and
corners of the quarto pages. It must have
required some courage to face the document in
the way of trying to master it ; he feared lest
it might prove too much for his fair disciple,
and he wrote again, " I have some more Greek
to send you as soon as I can get time to trace
the long scrawl which I have prepared. I
would like to know how you like the previous
dose, wherein you found my notes helpful to
you, if you did so at all, and wherein they
puzzled instead of instructing you." He then
breaks off into French, of which the following
sentences are very like himself :—" Mais, ma
chère, ne vous ennuyez trop de ces études ; la
critique Biblique est bien utile, mais c'est
l'Esprit qui vivifie.—Il n'y a point besoin de
vous resouvenir de soulager les pauvres ; vous
le faites sans cesse." But she had not been
discouraged by the " dose," for she answered,
" As for Greek, I find your notes very interesting and very helpful to me. You make the
thing appear simpler to me and more easy to
be attained than I at first supposed." She
very fully reciprocates the religious sentiments
that abound in his letters, of which the following is an example :—" I pray to see in the
promises the riches of the Father's love, the
value of the Son's obedience, and the mighty
power of the Spirit's operation. I must have
them or I die. I had fainted if I had not be-

lieved to see the goodness of the Lord in the
land of the living; and I am often at the
nearest (or very near) point to fainting through
not believing. Oh how bitter are the fruits of
sin, and when they are felt how sweet the con-
solations of God! Oh meditate on the promises,
pray with regard to each promise, ' Good is the
mind of Jehovah; be it unto me as Thou hast
said.' Not one good word shall fail; only believe, hope, wrestle, wait."

One sentence, however, was afterwards remarkably untrue, for he writes: "I am not
much in the habit of complaining to my fellow-
creatures about religious matters or anything
else." The habit of complaining to his fellow-
creatures about religious matters grew upon
him and continued to his dying day; but from
first to last he might certainly say, as very few
men could, "I am not much in the habit of
complaining about anything else."

In 1838 Mrs. Duncan had a daughter,
named Annie, who afterwards went with Mr.
and Mrs. Allan to the island of St. Thomas,
where her mother was born. She was married
there to Mr. Leckie, and died, leaving two
children, a son and daughter. Mrs. Duncan
died in Glasgow after the birth of a second
daughter, who only breathed and died, and of
whom he used to say most tenderly, "I can
trust even for my unbaptized infant." Widowed
of one in every way worthy of him, he mourned
his own great loss in the full assurance of her
everlasting gain. Taking a friend with him to
look at the dead body, he stood over it, and

without uttering more, he repeated with thrilling solemnity the words of our Shorter Catechism : " The souls of believers are at their death made perfect in holiness, and do immediately pass into glory ; and their bodies, being still united to Christ, do rest in the grave till the resurrection."

CHAPTER IV.

MISSION TO THE JEWS IN HUNGARY.

The Dust of the Earth is on the throne of the Majesty on
High.—J. D.

IN 1841, Dr. Duncan was appointed by the
Church of Scotland as a missionary to the Jews
in the beautiful city of Buda-Pesth, on the
Danube ; the handsome town of Pesth on one
side, and the ancient and Eastern-looking Buda
on the other, with the broad river flowing
between, and its humble bridge of boats in
process of being modernized into an elegant
bridge of iron. Twenty years later, after
passing with him along that bridge to Buda,
he turned to an old stone image of Christ in
his sufferings, and said to me, " Each time I
pass that rude stone it melts my heart;" this
was recalling his former residence in Pesth.
Another association, belonging rather to his
later years, attaches itself to the Blocksberg,
the fortified hill which crowns Buda, and
looking over Pesth commands a wide view of
the vast plains of Hungary. In his older life
he contemplated death in a manner kindred to
the thoughts of some of our martyred fore-

fathers in their pathetic farewells to sun, moon, and stars, to the green earth and the blue sea. He felt that he had neglected the beauties of the world in which he had lived so long ; and in a visit to the country, where his attention had been frequently directed to the beauty of the evening skies, he said, " I 've got an extraordinary lesson here ; I 've learned to read the sunsets, God's sunsets." In the same train of thought he said, " Wherefore doth God so clothe the grass of the field ? would it not be as useful without so beauteous a dress ? In the wilderness, where no man is, what is the use ? It blooms. and blossoms in God's own eye, Himself delights in it." So in revisiting Pesth in 1862, he looked up to the Blocksberg, and said, " I am growing old, and feel that I cannot now be long here ; I would like to be on the top of that hill with its fine view, for this is a bonny world after all. I sometimes like to climb a hill, and sit down and look round on this beautiful earth, that I may carry away with me as much of it as I can, and may be able afterwards to remember what this world was like."

When in Glasgow, Dr. Duncan had received from Aberdeen the degree of LL.D., in acknowledgment of his Hebrew and Oriental learning. But during his long life none of our Universities were happy enough to make the discovery, that by numbering him with their divines they would have enriched the roll of their Doctors in Divinity with the name of a man unequalled in theology by any Scotchman of his own

E

generation, and beside whom other men seemed scarcely to be theologians.

Before leaving Scotland, he had been married again to a widow lady, Mrs. Torrance, who entered with Christian enthusiasm, energy, and wisdom into all his missionary work. Their house in Pesth was thrown open to the Jews; they saw all their habits and ways, and had Christianity presented before them without being forced upon them. His very peculiarities seemed to suit them, and to attract rather than to offend; and his truly Christian tact was so great, that his opponents spoke of him as "a very cunning missionary."

On their arrival in Pesth they found a number of English engaged in the erection of the chain bridge, and their presence gave the missionaries a legal opportunity of preaching the Gospel, of which they gladly availed themselves. Dr. Duncan was requested to marry two British subjects, and consented. A few days after he had performed the ceremony, the Archduke Palatine of Hungary sent for him, and after a kind reception told him that it was his duty to inform him that the act was illegal, and must not be repeated. He answered, "I am an ordained minister of the Established Church of Scotland, and I hold myself entitled under Christ to administer the ceremony of marriage between British subjects." The Archduke replied, "I don't question your ministerial orders, but marriage in this country is civil as well as religious, and must be administered by a clergyman recognised by law. But all that

I ask you to do is in future to act on such occasions as the vicar of a legally recognised pastor." Proceeding on his uniform breadth of view, and acting with his usual prudence, Dr. Duncan at once consented; and in baptism and every other ordinance, both he and our other missionaries to the Jews always acted as vicars to Pastor Török, the honoured super-intendent of the Reformed Church, from whom they invariably received the greatest kindness.

ROMAN CATHOLIC AND HEBREW DOCTORS.

Dr. Duncan's conscience was more alive than most men's to the evil of any conformity or countenance to the errors of Popery, and he would not be present even in the way of curiosity at the idolatrous service of the mass. When his friends went to witness the pomp of that worship in Rome on a high occasion he left them at the door of the church. But he could attend the preaching without scruple; he described with great vivacity the sermons which he heard in Italy; and in the Roman Catholic creed he always owned the "wheat" with which the "arsenic" was mingled. Of his remarkable intercourse in Pesth with the Hebrew and Roman Catholic doctors, Mr. Allan sends a graphic account. "For a while in Pesth it was a precious time. The great subjects of the Gospel were presented and defended as new. The venerated beliefs and positions of Judaism presented themselves in

numbers of living, intelligent men ; and the
discussion of these gave exercise to his beloved
acquirements of Hebrew and Latin. The latter
he spoke with great purity, precision, and
readiness ; the effort that he required to make
to find and frame his words gave compactness
to his discourse ; when he had to quote Scripture it behoved to be in the original, as such
is the practice of the Jews, and only so is it
of authority. Such engagement kept mind,
body, and spirits healthy ; prayer too, active ;
and the fruit was seen.

" It was at this time that, besides daily converse with learned Jews and Roman Catholics,
numbers of both attended his Sabbath services.
Among the latter was a company of four
friends, three of them priests, and one a young
lawyer. The eldest of the priests had the
honorary office of Chaplain to the King of
Sardinia ; another of them has appeared pro-
minently in the Council at Rome, Sr Ludo-
vicus Waynald, Bishop of some place in Croatia,
I think. Among their other duties they conducted a newspaper in Magyar, and at that
time the controversy was very keen between
them and Protestant Rationalists. Of course
the Catholics were too wise, I may say too
faithful, to take their stand upon any accretions ;
they stuck to the fundamental verities.   ' I,'
said the Doctor, openly and repeatedly, ' side
with the Catholics." He could not then read
Magyar ; but he used to see both papers on
the controversy, and count the passages of
Scripture quoted by each.   ' I find,' said he,

' that the Catholics quote Scripture six times for the Protestants' once.' Our friends attended our Sabbath services most regularly ; the Doctor preached a series of discourses on the Lord's Prayer ; they were very anxious to have these discourses to publish in their paper, but you know how impossible that was in the absence of a shorthand writer. One thing was very marked in his public and private intercourse with these gentlemen and others of the same church : he always guardedly spoke of the church as the ' *Western Church.*' I understood it to be a compromise between Catholic and Roman. I remember the great surprise expressed by my young friend of the priests in these words : ' But your doctor is orthodox.'

" These things recall very pleasant memories. Our four friends wished to learn English (as England at that time was the model set up by the Hungarians), and I was their teacher. It opened for me much pleasant intercourse. Would that it had been more profitable. I spent some days with Waynald at Gran, where he was Professor of Theology, and had the honour of being introduced to the Prince Primate. I am sure my then master, Dr. Duncan, would not have objected to any respect showed the venerable man, or any received from him. Dr. Duncan said he would preach in the Pope's pulpit if he asked him, and I feel sure that he would have done it with surpassing delicacy.

" It was toward the close of this happy time

that we used to have the communion in an upper room ; joined with others by a venerable Countess Brunswick, a single lady with one maid-of-all-work, a devout Catholic clinging to the hope of reformation in her venerated Church. Schauffler and family visited us about the same time on their way from Vienna, where he had been printing his Bible. Old Saphir had for some time been often with us in public and private ; leading (or being led, you could hardly tell which) by the hand his Benjamin, Adolph. He was present as a witness on that occasion of our communion to which I refer. I can never forget *that* sight. He was sitting on a chair ; the boy, standing, was between his knees, the young head reaching nearly to the aged face, the face nearly resting on the youthful head. We had ended the Supper. Dr. Duncan gave out the 64th Paraphrase, ' To Him that loved the souls of men.' To our surprise the voice of the old Hebrew rose above our voices, and when we looked to him the tears were falling plentifully on the head of Adolph. These are days to be remembered."

" The Dust of the Earth on the throne of the Majesty on high " [5] was the great stumbling-block to those Israelites ; yet some of them were learning to " call Jesus Lord."

FRUITS OF THE MISSION.

The venerable Saphir, one of the most respected Jews in Pesth, and his whole family

with him, were among the first fruits of the
mission. The boy, on whose head his old
father's tears fell so fast, has long been well
known as one of the most devoted, honoured,
and successful of the Presbyterian ministers in
England. Two Hebrew students, afterwards the
Rev. Mr. Edersheim of Torquay and the Rev.
Mr. Tomory of Constantinople, were among the
earliest converts. Of his daily intercourse
with them and others in the freshness of their
first love Dr. Duncan spoke afterwards with
interest and enthusiasm. In reading the New
Testament with them, they found it speak so
exactly to their own circumstances, their joys,
their hopes, their difficulties, their trials, that
he said to me, " They used to read day after
day the Epistles of Paul, as if they had been
letters that had come by that morning's post."
In this city more than a hundred Hebrew converts have since been baptized in the name of
" Him whom the nation abhors."

Our missionary to the Jews in Constantinople, the Rev. Alexander Tomory, himself
one of the first fruits of the mission to Pesth,
sends an interesting account of Dr. Duncan's
work there, and at the same time pays an
affectionate tribute to the memory of his devoted wife :—" While the Church at home
made preparation for her work among the children of Israel, and fixed on Pesth as her first
central mission, the Lord prepared some souls
in that dark land to be the first recipients
of these bounties, the first fruits of the great
gathering, the trophies of his redeeming love.

If my time permitted I would gladly prepare
a full statement as a tribute of filial love
and affection towards him who, in the providence of God, was to me as a father, at
whose feet I gladly sat, and whose teaching
and godly example were so much blessed to
me.

"Six hours distant from Pesth sighed a lonely
soul for the Word of life. In vain did I speak
to Protestant theological professors and Roman
Catholic bishops; they had nothing to say to
lead an erring sheep back to the great Shepherd; but a high prelate in Vienna on hearing
my story said, 'Why did you come here? in
Pesth there are English missionaries.' So
these functionaries there had notice of Dr.
Duncan's presence in the capital of Hungary,
and three days later I was introduced to the
dear man. In a most syllogistic way, and in
fluent Latin, he brought out the truth of the
Gospel, and urged me to accept of Christ as my
Saviour. I well remember the time and the
locality; the very words still linger within me
with a thrilling echo. But quite in keeping
with the character of the Doctor, with the
ruling passion, in the same breath he began to
teach me English. While the tears were yet
in my eyes and in his he began to conjugate
an English verb, and made me repeat it. After
that I saw him almost daily till he left for
Italy. That was in November 1842. He left,
but the blessing remained behind. It was a
time of love, a time of the right hand of the
Most High; it was a pentecostal time. I have

seen for months a large hall filled with Jews twice a week, drinking in the words as they came from Messrs. Smith and Wingate. It was a time of earnest prayer, and souls were born as in a day. Two or three met together, and spent whole nights in prayer; they prayed for the missionaries, for the work, for individual souls, and for Israel in general, and surprising answers were granted.

" When he returned to Pesth in June 1843, I was already baptized, and a number besides. He was surrounded by a flock of new-born souls, and felt quite overwhelmed. I well remember his English sermon, preached on the first Sabbath after his return, on III John 3, ' I rejoiced greatly when the brethren came and testified of the truth that is in thee, even as thou walkest in the truth.' He was deeply moved and scarcely able to proceed. The words of Cæsar might be applied to him in a spiritual sense, *Veni, vidi, vici.* Whole days were occupied in receiving visitors, and his metaphysical and conversational powers were brought into full play. I heard him talking away for hours together on the most abstruse questions; we hung on his lips, and drank in every word. A Popish priest, Professor in the Theological Seminary, called one afternoon, and the discussion was a most animated one. The Doctor brought out glorious truth in most classic Latin, and the Professor seemed to enjoy it immensely, although opposing the propositions advanced. His learning attracted many people; Rabbis, teachers, and students

were daily visitors; there was a constant
coming and going, and the regular instruction
was almost left entirely to Messrs. Smith
and Wingate. His influence in the place
was immense, and he certainly used it for
good.

" He greatly desired the revival of the Hungarian Church; various plans and means were
proposed, but to this day, I am afraid, with
very little effect. It is in part owing to the
rationalism of the clergy and the strong influence of the laity. In the time of persecution
the Protestant nobles did immense service to
the Church; indeed they saved her as far as
human agency went, for they only could stem
back the rolling tide of persecution. In this
way they got all the power into their hand,
and they have used it for opposing the progress
of the Gospel, which they denounce as priest-
craft. This was the case during the time I
spent in Hungary from 1836-42; and from
what I saw and heard during my last visit
there, I am afraid the same influences with few
exceptions are still at work.

"There was another silent worker whose sweet
and powerful influence was felt by all—I refer
to the late Mrs. Duncan. She was devoted,
kind and affable ; well fitted for the important
position and the great opportunities which
the head of the Church vouchsafed to them.
Along with devotedness and piety she was
possessed of singularly good sense and practical
wisdom; well fitted in every way to be a mother
in Israel. She did great service to the Church

in taking care of the Doctor during his labours
in Pesth, and after he accepted the call for the
Professorship in Edinburgh. She took her full
share of the work and the responsibilities, and
very early we felt her kindness towards us.
She had a smile and a word of counsel for us
all. She was beloved by all, and very popular.
I will ever remember with thankfulness that
the Lord brought me into connexion with our
Church, and gave me the precious opportunity
of living under the roof of Dr. and Mrs.
Duncan. What many a minister owes to a
godly mother, the Lord granted me to enjoy
as a stranger in a strange land through the
kindness and the wisdom of that singularly
devoted mother in Israel. Dr. Edersheim, Mr.
Saphir, and myself, lived with them during the
first session after the Disruption. What a
heavy charge, to have three young inexperi-
enced youths to deal with! but her kind and
judicious dealings made it all easy. She had
an eye upon our comforts, upon our studies,
Scotticising us, and imbuing us with good
principles. Her influence over me was para-
mount. On standing a few months ago at
their silent graves, and when the memory of
the past rushed in upon me, I could not but
repeat the words of truth :—' The memory of
the just is blessed. And they that be wise
shall shine as the brightness of the firmament,
and they that turn many to righteousness as
the stars for ever and ever.' "

The pious Philip Saphir, an elder brother of
Adolph, being laid aside by want of health,

commenced in his sick-room a school for Jewish
children, which the Lord haṣ blessed beyond
all other Christian schools among the Jews.
For nearly thirty years, through every variety
of trial, and during the banishment of our
missionaries, it has endured and flourished.
It now possesses a large and beautiful building,
secured by the Government as the property of
our Scottish Church, and attended by about
500 children, nearly three-fourths of them
being Jews. They are admirably educated in
all respects, thoroughly taught in the New Testament as well as in the Old, and are always
much interested, often deeply impressed, with
the great truths of redemption. At the close
of the last annual examination in July 1872,
a learned Israelite, the director of one of the
Jewish schools in Pesth, said, " Sir, permit me
to express my deep sense of personal obligation for the excellent instruction my children
enjoy (three grandchildren are pupils). I must
also beg leave to say, as one who has made
school-work a study for many years, that I have
never witnessed anything to equal the results
of these days. The numerous branches taught
are handled with consummate skill, and the
answers of these children might well put young
men in our gymnasiums to blush. The love
and patience also of your teachers are to me as
remarkable as their success. Truly they may
well have respect to a heavenly reward ; for
no amount of pecuniary remuneration could
adequately recompense them."

HUNGARIAN AND BOHEMIAN CHURCHES.

Dr. Duncan's large catholicity of heart led him not only to take a deep interest in the Protestant Continental Churches, but, when occasion offered, to act along with them in a way that greatly furthered both Christian intercourse and the cause of Christ. Both in Hungary and Bohemia the Reformed Church was by far the more numerous, and its principles being more nearly akin to his own, it naturally attracted him most strongly ; but in both countries the Lutheran Church had also a firm place in his heart.

He pressed and brought into operation, if he did not suggest, a provision of bursaries to enable Hungarian and Bohemian students, in whom he took the liveliest and most affectionate interest, to attend our theological hall. Between him and a number of the pastors in Hungary and Bohemia there was the closest friendship, with a very warm mutual affection. Yanata and Schubert in Bohemia, were as dear to him as Török and Bauhoffer in Pesth. Before his last visit to these countries he was amusingly anxious to have himself photographed for the sake of his foreign friends, and was afterwards most careful to present them with his portrait. On the other hand, it was most pleasant to see how unfeignedly they honoured him, and how ardently they loved him ; they cherished toward him at once an unbounded respect as to a father, and an intense affection as to a brother, and by none in his own country was his loss more sincerely lamented. He studied their 'languages with great zeal, and they have been most anxious to present an account of his life both in Hungarian and Czech. Throughout his last years the welfare of their churches had a very large portion of his interest in the Church of Christ on earth. Spain and Italy shared in that interest.

HUNGARIAN PATRIOTISM.

Dr. Duncan entered with great warmth into the national feelings of the Hungarians, although his more immediate object was apart from them. He liked to repeat the Magyar proverb : " Nisi in Hungaria, non est vita ; si vita, non est ita." (There is no life except in Hungary ; if life there be, it is not such life.) He thoroughly sympathized with their love of liberty ; for he could not endure oppression of any kind, individual or national, and he kindled into a fierce blaze of indignation in speaking of Kossuth and the " oppressed nationalities."

The Protestant Magyars he liked all the more for their Calvinist creed, and said of them in our General Assembly, " The Magyars would die for Calvinism ; I wish I could add that they will live it." In 1849, during the Hungarian conflict with Austria, he wrote to his son-in-law in Constantinople : " We had a letter a few days ago from an English gentleman, a ship-builder at Alt-Ofen, who had arrived in England, having at last made his escape, with his whole family, from the seat of war. He anxiously inquires about the Rev. Messrs. Bauhoffer, Szecacs, and Török, who had gone along with the Hungarian army, and wishes me to mention them to you, and to inquire if you have heard anything of them, as they may not improbably find their way into Turkey. It would be right that you should keep a look-out if any of them make their appearance in Constantinople, or anywhere else in the Ottoman dominions, in which you could directly or indirectly be helpful to them. I am confident that you would do anything in your power to assist these worthy persons. Poor Kossuth! if *he* or any of the fugitives come your way, or where you have the least influence, you will show all respect and kindness to the oppressed patriots. Alas for the Magyar-Arság, trampled down at last under the feet of the oppressor! the day of thy restoration may yet arrive."

His emotions on all occasions were apt to be irrepressible, and their expression was sometimes inconvenient. When he revisited Hungary in 1862 the national jealousy towards Austria had considerably abated, but was still strong enough to prompt the question to a stranger, " Aimez-vous l'Autriche ou la Hongrie ?" In sailing down the Danube from Vienna, when we neared the Hungarian border, but had not reached it, he stood fixed by the ship's side intently observing the shore. Suddenly he took off his hat in the midst of a crowd of passengers preparing to land; and

with as loud a voice as he could utter, he
shouted a trumpet-like " *Viva!*" that startled
them all, and kindled suspicious and very angry
looks in two or three gentlemen with high-
crowned hats, who stood close beside him and
might be Austrian officials. He had descried
the Hungarian colours, the red, white, and
green of the national flag; and broke out into
this outburst of joy and welcome, which made
us for the moment shy of identifying ourselves
with him in his Magyar zeal.

But we soon found that we had passed the
border by other tokens besides the colours on
the bank of the river and the thrilling shout
of our Hungarian comrade ; for the whole
aspect on deck was now very different from
what it had been on leaving Vienna. The
captain had changed his dress, and clothed
himself in the picturesque garb of Hungary ;
out of a crowd of German or English hats that
had sailed with us in the morning, our own
were the solitary specimens left ; the other
passengers all wore the round, broad-brimmed
felt hat of Hungary. The high-crowned hat
had been an attestation of true loyalty in
Vienna, and in its absence the Custom-house
officers were instructed to be more careful in
their scrutiny ; but the wearers of this badge
had all either themselves disappeared at land-
ing-places in the Austrian territory, or just as
our vessel was about to enter the Hungarian
waters, or else they had been provided with a
change of hats for the now altered nationality.
Dr. Duncan amused us with telling that his

son-in-law, Mr. Allan, had been the only owner of an English hat in Damascus, and that the Damascenes had named him, in genuine Eastern phrase, " The son of the chimney-pot ;" and for the moment we thought nothing of finding ourselves the sole surviving " sons of the chimney-pot" on board.

In the evening, however, as we approached Pesth, one of the soldiers in the ship accosting us kindly and respectfully, said, " Gentlemen, you cannot go ashore with those hats !"—not of course on account of the authorities, but from the strong anti-German feelings of the people. At this warning, to use an expression of our friend's, " we looked dismal foolish ;" for, excepting a youth with his Highland bonnet, we had only our English hats. One of our number, with characteristic determination and independence, would not brook that any nation should displace his English crown, but wore it all our time in Pesth at the cost of occasional insult as " a low German." Dr. Duncan took enthusiastically the opposite course, and walked bareheaded with the obnoxious hat in his hand through the crowd on the wharfs. Afterwards, in the hotel, he would not let us rest till we had gone to a hatter and attired ourselves nationally. His was the wiser way, for we had found the waiters very heedless of our wants, and had difficulty in getting what we asked to eat ; but all were pleasant and obliging when we returned with the constitutional low-crowned felts.

CALL TO SCOTLAND.

In 1842 the state of Dr. Duncan's health was such that he was ordered to a warmer climate, and was sent as a missionary to the Jews in Leghorn. There was little direct fruit of the mission, yet on his work and his English preaching there he always looked back with much interest ; but he was glad when he was permitted to return to Pesth after the winter.

The Disruption in the Church of Scotland in 1843 suddenly altered all his plans and the course of his life. Along with all the other missionaries he threw in his lot, not only decidedly, but ardently and joyfully, with the ministers and people at home who formed themselves into the Free Church, that in things spiritual they might be subject only to Christ. He had long desired to occupy the Chair of a Professor of Hebrew. He believed that he could thus best of all serve the cause of missions to the Jews, and in accepting the mission he had distinctly stated that he would hold himself at liberty to receive such a call. The Free Church of Scotland had no hesitation in appointing him their first Professor of Hebrew and Oriental Literature, he had no hesitation in accepting their unanimous call, and accordingly he returned to Edinburgh before the beginning of winter, to engage in the new duties which were to occupy him for the rest of his life.

CHAPTER V.

Men should be living like dethroned Princes: that is but half the truth: Believers should be living like restored Princes.—J. D.

"MANY will be wishing you a happy New Year at this time : Gentlemen, I wish you a happy Eternity," was his opening salutation to his students at the beginning of a year soon after his induction into the Hebrew Chair of the New College ; [8] and its tone was characteristic of all his teaching during the twenty-seven years of his life in Edinburgh.

THE HEBREW CHAIR.

No place in life would have exactly fitted Dr. Duncan ; there was no calling which he could have exercised as efficiently as an ordinary man ; his seven talents were indeed singularly productive in their own way, yet his outward place might have been better occupied by a man with two. As a minister he was commonly too abstruse except for a peculiar audience, although no man could be so sublimely simple ; as a missionary he was too impulsive for permanent work, although there has seldom been such a missionary when his whole heart and intellect were in the mission; as a professor he was unequal to the ordinary round of little duties, while he was apt to be carried away with what was more extremely little because secondary and remote in the study, yet scarce any man knew his subject so well or loved it so much. It was not that he disliked teaching, for he was passionately fond of it; nor was it exactly that he disrelished duty merely as such, when it became regular and formal and same, as all duty partially becomes. Duty, law, conscience were theoretically far higher with him than with other men, more admired and more revered; and in heart he loved their practice as few men could love it. But he failed in the ordinary daily round, partly because he was often carried away intellectually with some engrossing mental interest, or carried away spiritually by an absorbing love of God, or a fearful inquiry into his own standing before Him. But that was not all; there was also a singular weakness of purpose in common things. His feebleness of mind was about as marked in this respect as his intellectual vigour otherwise; he has been called, and truly, a giant in intellect and a child in humility; but he was a child also in weakness of will in ordinary matters. That he could be easily diverted from the drudgery of common duties, was a sin; but it was a mental weakness as well, for it did not adhere to duties specially, but to any ordinary matters whatever. In any practical matter thought of or proposed by himself or by others, or for himself or for others, you could not name any living man whom you could so easily turn aside in judgment from what he had approved, or in execution from what he had intended, through excessive weakness of purpose in little things, or in great things that were not outstanding. In this respect he was not merely childlike but childish. His irregularity in work was not mostly a shrinking from a disrelished drudgery; but seemed to be the result of an extreme constitutional weakness of will, which it was really hard, and which he found it impossible, to overcome.

But there was no sphere where what was most valuable in Dr. Duncan could have been brought out more profitably than in the Hebrew Chair. After a time his defects as a teacher were more than supplied by the appointment of a coadjutor, Dr. Davidson, first as assistant and then as colleague, whose qualifications he always valued as of the very highest order; and his position as professor gave him an audience, many of whom learned from him lessons of life-long value both for themselves and as teachers of others. Intellectually, theologically, exegetically, and spiritually, many of his students learned from him what few men in a generation are able to communicate. In the highest subjects of human concern they heard thoughts of genius, great in themselves, and still more precious as the germs of other thoughts of their own ; they came in contact with attainments in learning which both opened new views of the vastness of the field, and set before them an example of what might be reached ; but above all they saw genius and learning, not merely made handmaids to grace, but evidently and utterly " counted loss for the excellency of the knowledge of Jesus Christ." They saw a man of the highest intellect, one of the first among the wise, becoming a babe ; and not teaching them as scholars, but babelike thirsting for and drinking the milk of the Word, and so moving them to thirst and drink for themselves. Beyond all calculation must have been the benefit, both doctrinal and spiritual, to many now ministers of the Gospel, and through them to their flocks.

"At the prayer-meeting of the students attending the new College," writes one of our ministers, " what I felt of great benefit then and since was the setting forth with such clearness the Person of Christ, as the grand and glorious embodiment of the whole Gospel and truth of God. This has given me a basis and firm foundation for all Gospel preaching, and has proved a sheet anchor against all error ; and this, I believe, has tended to revive the power and popularity of Gospel preaching in our day. It is twenty-six years since I listened to those addresses, but the truth seems as distinct and impressive as when I listened to them." [1]

" He came one day to the class," writes another, " utterly broken and dejected. He said, 'Here I am; and I have not a single idea,' and asked a student to pray. He said that the reason of his constraint was that the day before they had applauded him too much. He felt at the time that it was wrong. When they ruffed he had raised his hand by way of remonstrance; but he had not protested with sufficient energy against it. They had given him and he had taken something of the honour due to God alone. The Lord had rebuked him by taking away all his ideas."

In personal conversation with his students he spoke to them with great faithfulness. His own humility and his extreme self-condemnation disarmed all jealousy of his sitting in judgment on them. In a number of instances within my own knowledge he pressed on students for the ministry the question, " Have you been born again?" with a directness that could not be turned aside, yet with such tenderness that his faithfulness never gave offence.

His pre-eminent fitness for the Hebrew Chair in point of learning, and his practical defects in the want of methodical habits, are both brought out by Mr. Allan in the following notes :—

" His Hebrew and Oriental scholarship you all know and admit, but perhaps not to its full extent as compared with other scholars. Schauffler is a very competent witness, both from his own immense practical attainments and his conversational and literary use of these tongues, and also from his personal acquaintance with the German masters. I have heard him say that Gesenius was not to be compared with Dr. Duncan for the deep accurate knowledge of the sacred tongue. I am happy to think that, though he left nothing written, he has conveyed to others who appreciated and will perpetuate his keen valuable observations, if not discoveries, on the Grammar of the Hebrew. We all know his extensive and accurate acquaintance with the vocabulary of the Hebrew Bible, and the rich use he made of it, though in his own studies, and specially in his teaching he left that for less practical points. For instance, his pupils will remember what time was devoted, when he took the notion, to the system of punctuation (accents) which he formed into a scale illustrated by his fingers and their different joints. I remember well the weary, fruitless days spent by him and me in trying to learn the musical value of the accents, according to the Portuguese Synagogue, taught, or rather tried to be taught, us by old Lyon. Dr. Duncan had no ear for music, and I have about as little, but he thought otherwise. So the arrangement was that I should learn the music from our instructor, and by longer practice than we could afford to pay for, or may be longer than the old chanter had patience to stay, I should convey it to him. It was a hopeless task, on account of the pupil and tutor. I have a copy, the only copy I ever saw, of the accents set to musical punctuation, at the welcome service of any one who wishes it.

" His failure in teaching was a great burden to his wife ; what efforts she made to keep him to some regularity, keeping a catalogue of the names of the students, telling him once every morning what names to call, receiving their exercises, seeing that they were reviewed and returned in proper order and time, you will know better than I. He was carried on by impulse in selecting his subjects, or rather made no selection, but was carried away by the subject that presented itself; and he pressed it without regard to its importance, the stage of his scholars, and especially without regard to the capacity to take in, far less to digest the mass. I saw a pupil get all the thirteen conjugations of the Arabic verb in one lesson, and followed into his bedroom with additional matter; three times that night was there an additional lesson, the last about three o'clock in the morning."

SPIRITUAL INFLUENCE.

In his sayings published in his Life, there is one that stands alone; it is his comment on the Scriptural words, " The prince of the power of the air:"—" I think the air is figurative; we talk of breathing a bad moral atmosphere, and I think there is a very bad air just now. I remember once, when in a state of poverty of soul, of an air coming from the Word of God, it was not any particular place, just air to breathe in." These words bring out a most characteristic feature, not peculiar to himself in kind, but very special in degree; and one that is so faintly marked in most men as to be scarcely appreciable. His mental instinct was such that he not only saw things mental with singular clearness, but almost seemed to see mind itself ; and his spiritual instinct gave him a rare sensitiveness to the spiritual " air " that surrounded him.

His spiritual receptivity, and still more its converse in the influence of his spirit over the spirits of others, are brought out in the following incident. Readers will receive it differently, and some will set it aside as a mere imagination ; but the fact remains simply as I relate it. In its own character it belongs to the things of which it is written, " Hast thou faith ? have it to thyself before God ;" and they are nothing to other men. Partly on this account, and partly because I had found it impossible to eliminate myself, I deleted the incident after it was in print ; but on second thoughts have restored it. In the memorials of most men it would have fallen to be left among thoughts that may be spoken, but are best unwritten ; but it is desirable that a man so numbered by himself among men should be seen and surveyed on every side. It occurred after his return from Pesth in 1844 ; and, although merely an incident in his life, was an event in mine, because it connected his future path with my own.

All who are in the habit of leading in social prayer know how sensibly the petitions of the speaker are influenced by the spirits of those who silently aid in the exercise, and how real and practical in this relation is that " communion of saints " in which we believe. But such communion is seldom brought out in so definite and marked a manner as it was in this instance. Dr. Duncan's spiritual state was apt to be unequal; but when in spiritual vigour he had a singular insight into the spiritual world around him, a quick and very elevated sympathy with its movements, and a great power over the minds of others. That summer he spent some months with his young Hebrew converts in Pesth for the furtherance of their faith, and his own spirit was greatly refreshed by the intercourse. When he was a minister in Glasgow we were on terms of intimate friendship, but after his call to our Hebrew Chair in Edinburgh I had seen little of him. He lived in a distant part of the town, and never attended my church, not even once to my knowledge. This summer he had passed in Pesth, and from my connexion with our Committee on the Conversion of the Jews, I knew, or rather I believed as certainly as if I had known, that he had not yet returned to Scotland.

In church one Sabbath, in the progress of the morning prayer, I became gradually, but at length clearly and definitely, conscious that my thoughts and words were flowing in a channel that was not indeed alien to my intentions, but was distinctly different from any previous conceptions of my own. The impulse of a sensible force seemed increasingly to move me onward, but after a time one petition after another filled me with wonder. As they came up in succession I thought at last, " How is it that I am praying to-day in this manner? These thoughts are not my own thoughts, and the words that clothe them are words I never used before, nor thought of using. They are Dr. John Duncan's; it seems as if he were praying in me, for both the ideas and the language are his and not mine. He must be here, yet he never comes to this church; and he cannot be here, for he is in Hungary." Bewildered how it could be, but confident that he was in the church, I bent over the pulpit as soon as I had finished the prayer, and saw him close under me in the session seat. The mystery was solved clearly to me, although remaining mysterious for those who doubt all mystery. Dr. Duncan had entered the church after the commencement of the service, and in the exercise of his spirit there had surely been more than a merely passive following of the supplications that were pouring themselves through my lips.

At the close of the service I found him "full of faith and of the Holy Ghost," and under a more powerful and subduing impression than I had ever seen him before. He had arrived in town, I believe, on the previous evening, and had come to live nearer to my church. As soon as we were in the session-house, he said to me with deep emotion, " I could not help coming to this church this morning. It seemed to me that the Spirit was here, and that He drew me irresistibly to the place. I believe there is such a thing as the local presence of the Spirit." On pressing him afterwards on the expression, " a local presence of the Spirit," he declined to open it further, and only added, " I can't make it plainer than I have said, but I think I can make it out both from Scripture and from analogy."

From that morning he sat with us constantly, and was most regular and exemplary in his Sabbath attendance. For twenty years he was one of our elders, took a deep interest in all our affairs, was eminently profitable in religious conference in the kirk-session, always assisted at the Communion, and frequently preached on other occasions. During the first winter after his return from Pesth he preached in St. Luke's Church on the Sabbath evenings a series of admirable lectures ; and in returning from his funeral I met two friends who reminded me of them and said, " Those lectures, twenty-five years ago, were as fresh in their memories as if delivered yesterday." They were well attended, but when he concluded them at the end of the winter, he remarked to me, " I was never popular for more than six months at a time."

At this period of his life his great desire was to break up the surface religion both of self-called and of sincere Christians. Some years later he entered with all his might into the awaking of the world out of death ; but now his whole heart was set upon the awaking of the Church out of sleep. The " hypocrisy " of the name to live, over the stagnation and all but the corruption of death, which had been so terribly disclosed to him in Aberdeen two years

after his conversion, and " the coldish admiration of Christ," which he felt creeping over
him in Glasgow, he also saw prevailing in the
Church.   This complacent security he denounced as Antinomian ; not that it rested on
a doctrine verbally Antinomian, or resulted in
a walk openly sinful ; but it consisted with a
conscience very partially alive to the holiness
of God, the sinfulness of sin, and the unchangeable demands of the law, " Thou shalt love thy
God with all thy heart, and thy neighbour as
thyself."   There was no depth or duration of
doubt that he did not prefer to this carnal
confidence, which he set himself most resolutely
to dash in pieces ; intent only to break down
the pretentious evil, and leaving it to the Lord
to rebuild the purified truth in the hearts and
lives of his people.   " A ' perhaps' of salvation," he said, " works more in some souls
than all the fulness of the Gospel in others."
The preaching of " repentance toward God,"
as addressed to the Church as well as to the
world, he earnestly insisted on ; and often repeated the words, " Except ye repent ye shall
perish."   " If there were universal salvation,"
he said, " there would be universal repentance."
He was jealous of taking one half of a text
and leaving out the other, the practical half, as
in repeating the words, " As many as I love, I
rebuke and chasten," and omitting the rest,
" Be zealous therefore and repent."   He was
afraid of believers feeding on the promises and
neglecting the precepts of the Bible.   " Why
make a book," he asked, " out of a collection of

the promises? Why not as well make a collection of the precepts into a book?"

THE GOSPEL.

Notwithstanding the sternness of his earlier doctrine, and his life-long severity against himself, his preaching was full of consolation; and during the long period of his latter years he was both large-hearted in his views of what constitutes a child of God, and most free in the offer of the Gospel. After an address on the tokens of regeneration, he said to me with a quiet smile, "A man may want the marks you have given us, and be a true believer after all;" and of Thomas Sheppard, a severe sifter of sincerity, he said, "Sheppard's books are fine books for basketing the fish (Matt. xiii. 47, 48); but mind you must catch them before you basket them.—Sheppard is fine, but I wish I were as good as one of his hypocrites." That warrant for a free invitation, "Let him that heareth say, Come," was a favourite text with him, and often on his lips. His own cast of preaching was not that of an evangelist; yet night after night, and one year after another, he sat with delighted interest to hear Evangelists addressing crowds, and preaching chiefly the judgment to come, and a present acceptance of Christ with immediate joy in salvation. With such preaching he found no fault, provided it did not deny human inability, the Divine sovereignty, and the warrant and duty of prayer on the part of all men.

The true urgency of the Gospel he expressed in these words : " It will not do to tell a man that he *may* come to Christ, but that he *must* come, and that he *cannot* come ; that he must come, or he will look to another to come for him ; and that he cannot come, or he will look to himself for salvation." With all his theology no man was less trammelled by theological systems, either lax or severe ; less fettered by narrowness, as against the true breadth of Bible doctrine ; or more alert and frank to meet every human heart in every step of its return God-ward. And few men were so tender to inquirers, so hopeful in the first symptoms of a saving change, or more free in presenting Christ for universal and immediate acceptance. He repeated with the most cordial approval a remark which he had heard from the pulpit—on the words, ' All things are ready, go out into the highways, and as many as ye find, bid to the marriage '—that " the Gospel is a prepared feast for unprepared guests."

While he insisted much on the work of the Spirit, and on the utter incapacity of the natural man to discern or receive spiritual things, no man held more strongly that the necessity of conviction of sin by the Holy Spirit in no way interferes with the free offer of the Gospel. " If only convinced sinners," he said, " are warranted to embrace Christ, then I must, ere I can be warranted to embrace Him, be convinced that I am a convinced sinner. But the Holy Spirit is the only source

of infallible conviction, and the Holy Spirit is
nowhere promised to convince of conviction ;
he is only promised to convince of sin. True,
the convinced sinner is the only ' subjectum
capax ' (capable subject) of saving faith, but it
is not as a convinced sinner I am called upon
to come to Christ." [14]—" The Gospel does not
address convinced sinners as such with offers
of reconciliation, but *fallen* sinners. It is a
very beautiful arrangement in the Gospel that
it does not proclaim itself to convinced sinners.
None are so unwilling to consider themselves
convinced as those who really are. Every
unconvinced sinner imagines himself to be a
convinced sinner till the Spirit works in his
heart. But the convinced sinner would be the
last to embrace an offer made to convinced
sinners ; but proclaim the Gospel to a vile,
guilty sinner, and he saith, ' That is I.' [1]

" For myself, I cannot always come to Christ
direct, but I can always come by *sin*. Sin is
the handle by which I get Christ. I take a
verse in which God has put Christ and sin
together. I cannot always put my finger upon
Christ and say, ' Christ belongs to me ; ' but
I can put my finger upon sin and say, ' Sin
belongs to me.' I take that word, for instance, ' The Son of man is come to save that
which was lost.' Yes, lost, lost,—I 'm lost ;
I put my finger upon that word and say, ' I 'm
the lost one ; I 'm lost.' Well, I find that
' The Son of man is come to save the lost ; '
and I cry out ' What God hath joined together,
let not man put asunder.' "

G

As regards assurance, while he doubted so much for himself, there was none more prompt or skilful in removing the doubts of others; and while he was wont to look too much within for evidences, he held most clearly the immediate shining of Christ upon the soul, and the direct witness of the Spirit. In listening to an exposition of the text, "After ye believed ye were sealed with the Holy Spirit of promise," it was argued by the preacher that as the seal of the Spirit came "after" faith, it might be given at any time after it, and the believer might for long remain without it. Considering how strongly he held that believers may want assurance of salvation, I fully expected him to assent to the exposition; but he quite disagreed, and said, that "after" in these words did not at all imply an interval of time between the faith and its seal, but rather the one immediately following the other. He had a great jealousy for Jesus Christ, and of everything that would sever the light of the soul from the discovery of Christ. "'To you that fear my name shall the Sun of Righteousness arise with healing under his wings.' The healing is under the wings, it is not by itself; it is not Christ without benefits, or benefits without him, for the sun cannot be shorn of his beams. The way we obtain light is by the bright shining of the sun; and as soon may a man *bottle up day-light* as have a Gospel of benefits without the immediate shining of the Sun of Righteousness. As the old rays cannot be bottled up or preserved, so a believer cannot see light but in His shining, nor a dying sinner be raised up but by His shining." [1]

On our responsibility for carrying the Gospel to others, he said at one of our Communion tables : " Mind, you have got the sinner's Gospel, and if you have it, it is to give to sinners ; if you have it, you are a debtor to all the sinners to give it to them ; and then you have to be very nice, and let the sinners know that you are a sinner too when you give it to them, and that you have nothing else for yourself but that. Let us be sure to give it, lest if we do not give it, we do not get it : lest the Holy Ghost do not give it to us, if we keep it to ourselves. As being saved by the sinner's Gospel, God has made us Evangelists to the world."

THE LORD'S SUPPER.

" Many of the Old Testament saints," he said, " lived above their dispensation : most Christians live below theirs.—We make far too little of the *means* of grace : they are not grace, but they are the *media*, the middle things of grace, and that is much to us." He greatly prized the Sabbath ; and few men ever made so much of the preaching of the Word and all the means of grace, but especially of the Lord's Supper : " The great connecting link," he called it, " between the first and second coming of the Lord." Its dispensation was always to him a grand and high occasion, occupying his mind for many days before, and often for many days

or for weeks after. The magnitude and pre-
ciousness of the ordinance grew upon him
year by year, and in his latter years he was
usually bathed in tears at the Table. It was
deeply affecting to look on the holy man of
God weeping much because forgiven much. On
one occasion, while his own tears were flowing
freely in a mingled flood of joy and sorrow, he
heard a loud sob behind him, from a com-
municant who had come last to the Table, and
finding no room had been seated by the elders
close behind us. Turning round, and without
knowing "who or what manner of woman she
was" that so wept at the Lord's feet, he saw
her hand trembling to take the cup, and in a
loud and earnest whisper said to her, "It's for
a sinner." He spoke to a penitent Magdalene ;
himself in that hour among the chief of peni-
tents, loving much.

His convictions of sin often came with great
force at Communion times. On such occasions
he had commonly either a very deep impression
of sin or a very lively apprehension of Christ,
or both. Latterly he was simpler than at
an earlier period, and the thoughts of Christ
prevailed over the remembrance of sin. Once
when he had no liberty to communicate, and
had retired to the session-house, he met the
beadle, an intelligent and earnest Christian,
and asked him why he was not at the Table. He
told him his difficulties, which Dr. Duncan
answered, and then in his turn he asked the
Doctor why he was not there. The two had
a long discussion, each severely condemning

himself, and each persuading the other that he was wrong in the excessive self-condemnation, till in the end both prevailed, and both were overcome, and took their seats at the holy Supper.

At a Communion season, what is called the action sermon had been preached on the kingdom of heaven on earth, as an open market of salvation where everything may be freely bought which any man needs for eternal life, from the words of Isaiah : " Ho, every one that thirsteth, come ye to the waters ; come, ye, buy and eat ; yea, come, buy wine and milk without money, and without price." I feared to find him desponding, but with a countenance beaming with gladness he came up to me and said, " When I heard all the good things that were offered in this market, I said to myself, I will marry the Merchant and they will all be mine." At another time, when he was expected to take a Table service, but had been in doubt and difficulty about it, he rose up and began with the exulting words, " I shall not die, but live ;" and went on in a flow of heavenly eloquence, full of consolation to the pilgrim-guests of his well-beloved Lord. On some other occasions his face was glistening with joy at the sacramental feast.

The Lord's Supper, as a mere commemoration, was very far from meeting either his judgment or his affections ; his view of it was quite as sacramental as Calvin's, and he always looked on it as involving " a high mystery." At the close of a Communion service, he once said to me, " Your consecration prayer was not sacramental enough for me."

The value which he attached to this ordinance is brought out in a note by one of our ministers who served in the Crimean war. "At a Presbytery meeting for my trials for ordination to a Crimean chaplaincy, he exhorted me ; it was but in a word, but it struck me, nor did it pass without a protest by some member of the Presbytery : That I should not hesitate to administer the Communion to men dying on the field or in hospital, if I should see cause ; putting aside the protest to his suggestion by saying that the Lord in His providence might call me to do it, and there was nothing in our standards to prevent it." [7]

His Addresses at the Lord's Supper were often as long as ordinary sermons, but never diffuse or disjointed, and always engaging his entire energies of both mind and heart. For many years they were for the most part intensely theological, full of condensed thought in every clause, and occupied throughout with the person and sufferings of Christ in relation to the redeemed. Once he embodied in his address a very long and beautiful passage on the Person of Christ from one of the ancient Councils, with as much ease and precision as if he had been reading it, although he must have been both recollecting and translating it as he spoke. Except to a few, these noble meditations were too theological and intellectual for the occasion. But in his later years his Communion addresses underwent a great and almost incredible change. Without losing their loftiness, they were marked by an exquisite simplicity; they retained their terseness and power, but were touchingly tender, with a bright, continuous thread of scriptural truth running through them. Their most frequent close was, "Ye are bought with a price ; wherefore glorify God in your body and in your spirit, which are God's."

The following extract from notes taken in St. Luke's Church, at a Communion, nine years before his death, will serve to show the character of one of the sacramental addresses of his later years. "Methought the Lord showed me a heart into which he had put a *new* song; the soul was making melody, attempting to make melody to the Lord. Where it was I do not know, but I heard it singing about the middle of its song. It had been singing, 'What profit is there in my blood, when I go down to the pit?' It had been singing the fifty-first Psalm ; and Jehovah had put a new song into its mouth. He had done it, and it was trying to sing ; and I heard it in the middle of its song. It had been reading the fifth chapter of Revelation, and trying to sing some of its numbers; and now it was at these words, 'For Thou wast slain;' and oh how it was sobbing and breaking! how it was melting and breaking with a joyous grief and a grievous joy ! Oh how it faltered when it tried to sing, 'and hast redeemed us to God by thy blood.'

"It was the song of one to whom much had been forgiven, and who therefore loved much;

but it was the song of the chief of sinners, of one to whom *most* had been forgiven, and who therefore loved *most*. Yet it faltered and made wrong music; it jarred, and there was discord; and it grated on its own ear, and pained it; and God was listening to it, God who knoweth all things. But the song was presented through and by the Mediator of the new covenant; and if there was discord, it was removed by grace in atoning blood, by the sweet accents of intercession; for it came up as music in Jehovah's ear, melody to the Lord. It was not discord in heaven. I would know, O God, what soul that is; O God, let that soul be *mine!*"

In close connexion with the Lord's Supper, both in itself and in the constant exercise of his mind, is the following remarkable account of his deep entrance into the sufferings of Christ.

"In the winter of 1864, Dr. Duncan was reading part of Isaiah with his senior class. The particular passage I cannot remember, nor does it matter, for it only served as a suggestion of the cry in ver. 1 of the 22d Psalm, 'My God, my God, why hast thou forsaken me?' By the time Dr. Duncan had reached that point he had left his desk and, bent nearly double, was pacing up and down in front of the students' benches, his snuff-box and pocket-handkerchief in one hand, a huge pinch of snuff occupying the fingers of the other, but utterly forgotten in the absorbing interest of his subject, our Lord's sufferings for sinners, which he was turning over and looking at, now on this side, now on that, but all with a loving reverence, and as one who spoke in a half-sleeping vision, when suddenly a flash went through him as if heaven had opened. He straightened himself up, his face kindled into a rapture, his hand went up and the snuff scattered itself from the unconscious fingers as he turned to the class, more as it seemed for sympathy than to teach—' Ay, ay, d 'ye know what it was—dying on the cross, forsaken by His Father—d 'ye know what it was ? What ? What ?' (as if somebody had given him a *half* answer which stimulated him, but which he had to clear out of his way, a very usual exclamation of his when wrapped in thought.) ' What ? What ? It was damnation—and damnation taken *lovingly*.' And he subsided into his chair, leaning a little to one side, his head very straight and stiff, his arms hanging down on either side beyond the arms of his chair, with the light beaming from his face and the tears trickling down his cheeks he repeated in a low intense voice that broke into a half sob, half laugh in the middle, ' It was *damnation*—and he took it *lovingly*.' No saying of the many I have heard from him, nothing in all his manner and expression, ever struck me like this." [7]

PERSONAL CONVERSE.

The direct conversion of others bore a small proportion in his work for the Lord on the earth ; and after the first few years, of which I cannot speak, his preaching can scarcely be said to have very directly aimed at conversion.

But he spoke in personal conversation with great faithfulness. One of his students writes of him: " He was the only one of my teachers that ever spoke to me personally and directly regarding my spiritual state. When getting my certificate from him, he rose and paced the floor in silence for a little, then stood and looking kindly at me, asked, ' Do you believe in the necessity of regeneration ? ' ' Most certainly, Sir, I believe that no man can be a Christian unless he is born again.' ' Yes, I know that, but that is not what I mean : do you believe it necessary for a minister to be born again to preach the gospel ? ' " He was deeply concerned that his students should possess the great essential qualification for serving the Master. Many remember the lively interest he took in them in that respect.

He used to refer with much interest to the case of a woman who came to him in distress in the earlier part of his ministry. She was very slow in reaching a full conviction of her guilt and helplessness, and when at last she came to acknowledge this for herself, she still found no rest in Christ. He said, " She confessed herself to be the chief of sinners, but would not acknowledge that I was a sinner as well as herself. She stuck at the acknowledgment of her own sin, and she got no relief ; but the turning-point of light to her soul was when she came to allow me to say, I also am a sinner like yourself."

A case which he once took up he never forgot ; and he always remembered exactly what he had said, and resumed the conversation at the precise point where it had stopped. In calling one day at the house of one of my elders he found the family from home; but an old woman left in charge of the house received him kindly and gave him luncheon. Before leaving he spoke to her earnestly about salvation, but found her, as he said, " a Protestant Papist," making her religion her trust for eternity. She complained afterwards that he had said to her at last, " O woman, you are an unsaved sinner," which she thought very unkind after the kindness she had shown to him. A year later he said on his deathbed to his friend, " Many people are anxious to get rid of their doubts; but that old woman that keeps your house, it would be a great matter if you could get a doubt dinted (knocked) into her." Regarding impenitence at death he remarked: " I have more than once seen the calmness of the brutish ignorance of an unawakened conscience on the very verge of eternity. It was an awful calmness."

In cases of conscience his advice was most valuable; and he could be very freely consulted, for he entered into the inquirer's position with singular quickness of apprehension. " He had the tender unsophisticated conscience that is the best casuistry. Once, when the case was put whether one who had wronged another was bound not only to make restitution, but also to confess to the injured person, he said promptly, " He must confess. The mind is so constituted that without confession it cannot be at peace.

It may in certain cases be right to withhold
confession, when the interests of others are at
stake, never when our own only is concerned.
A man is not in a right state unless he is
willing, at any hazard to himself, to confess the
wrong. He can never be fully assured of his
willingness to confess till he has made confession. Hence till the wrong has been confessed settled peace of mind is impossible." [12]

While comparatively few may date their first
impressions of divine truth to Dr. Duncan's
teaching, the number is great of those who
have been indebted to that teaching for their
progress in the divine life, and for further
knowledge of the length and breadth of divine
truth. He often seemed to be occupied exclusively with his own spiritual condition, but
that never blunted his needle-like quickness of
perception regarding the state of the religious
world around him ; and he was peculiarly alive
to the danger of a semi-antinomian resting on
privilege and promise, apart from the present
activity of gracious affections and a daily progress in sanctification.

The sight of a man so thoroughly in earnest
in the Christian race, so deeply sensible of his
sins, and riveted so fast by the beauty of the
Lord Jesus Christ, was in itself to many one of
the best lessons in the divine life, one of their
strongest incentives to growth in grace, and
one of their greatest encouragements towards
attaining the full knowledge of Christ. The
pity which many good people felt for his
spiritual distress was often in so far misplaced

that he was not unacquainted with their state
of mind, and preferred his own darkness to
their light. An assurance of salvation founded
either on the fact of conversion, or on a present
faith in the Word of God, but not accompanied
or followed by corresponding spiritual affections and the present exercise of grace, would
have yielded no comfort to him.

Against the deceitfulness of sin he warned
his friends in such terms as these : " Sin says,
' I'm not sin at all.' Then Sin says, ' I'm
pleasant.' Yes, pleasant poison. Then Sin
says, ' Ah ! do you call that sin ? Well, it is
but a little sin.' Alas ! alas ! for us men there
can be no little sin, unless there be a little God
against whom to commit it. Then Sin says,
' It is a common sin ; good people do that.' A
good man has crooked legs ; are crooked legs
therefore no evil ? He has stiff joints ; are
stiff joints therefore no evil ? Ah ! men don't
argue that way about the natural evil, but they
do about the spiritual evil, because they love
sin, and will take any excuse for it, and never
readier than when they find it in a good man.
Then Sin says, ' If you sin there's Christ to go
to.' "

Again, he encouraged them to the conflict and
final triumph : "The Lord was not only David's
garrison, where he was safe from the attack,
but also his deliverer in the field. The Christian warrior must never make a truce ; he
may have to sound a retreat, but he must out
again ; the enemy is between him and the kingdom and the crown, and he must out again."[15]

SYMPATHY.

In describing Dr. Duncan we have once and
again quite unconsciously written down con-
tradictions ; to use his own expression, we have
written not mere " antinomies but antagon-
isms," which we have had to modify or explain
to keep within the limits of apparent truth.
Yet the real truth about him is often as near
a contradiction as is compatible with being
true. So it was in his world-wide sympathy,
a sympathy, not merely theoretic, but practical,
with all men. With all his want of common
sense in common things, yet when the whole
man was present, as on trying occasions abroad,
he put forth a consummate tact, and he showed
an unrivalled power of entering into other
men's sympathies. " Unto the Jews he became as a Jew, that he might gain the Jews ;
to the weak he became as weak, that he might
gain the weak ; he was made all things to all
men, that he might by all means save some."
In Pesth he so adapted himself to the Jews
that, as already noticed, his opponents re-
proached him as " a very cunning missionary,"
and friendly Jews spoke of him as entering
into their thoughts and feelings as no other
Gentile ever did. An Hungarian Jew told
me after his death, that Dr. Duncan and Dr.
M'Caul were the only Gentiles whom the Jews
regarded as thoroughly at home in their literature, and that our own Rabbi entered most
into the heart of the Jews.

For doctrinal truth, if it was gainsaid, he

would earnestly contend ; and not merely for
great truths, but also for the least, even to the
" straining out of the gnat" from the cup.
But in his largeness of sympathy with all men
he was quick, fertile, deep in finding out rally-
ing-points of agreement.   To the Jew he was a
child of Abraham ; to the Roman Catholic he
was an ancient churchman ; to the Armenian
in the East he would insist only on the words
of the Bible ; to the Hungarian he was in heart
a Magyar ; to the Bohemian a Czech ; to the
Highlander a Gael.   He learned all their languages, and entered so cordially into their sympathies, that they all loved him as they did
not love any other foreigner.

In circumstances of sorrow, in sickness, in
bereavement, in any affliction, he was not
merely kind, but with a kindness most discri-
minating and sympathetic.   " In affliction,"
he said, " mere natural human kindness is a
very valuable communication from the philanthropic God."   Toward the afflicted he showed
not only the tenderest pity, but the most delicate perception of the chords that ought to be
touched.

From the thoughts of a child his own
thoughts appeared to be commonly either soaring or sinking to the extremest distance ; yet
he could enter wondrously into a child's feelings, and he wrote a letter to his first grandson in which he seemed himself to become a
little boy again.   So also the summer before
his death, when his daughter from Philadelphia
was visiting him, he set himself with great

assiduity to teach her infant to walk, placing
chairs before the child, and persevering day by
day in his labour of love, till he had fairly
mastered the accomplishment of walking.   On
a visit to a friend he had spoken seriously to
the only child, a girl of six years of age ; but
after leaving the house he feared lest his words
might lose their effect, because in bidding
her farewell he had not entered into all the
sympathies of the child.   He hastened back,
at some inconvenience to himself, and having
found her, he said, " Let me kiss your doll
before I leave."   A mother said to her little
boy, " Here's Dr. Duncan ; you must be good."
" O yes," he broke in, " he'll be good ; but you
mustn't make a bogle o' me."   Again, in a girl
who had been brought up alone, he missed the
playfulness and hilarity natural to children.
One day he came with her to the house of another lady who had a child of her own age.
He said that all children ought to play ; that
he had noticed that she never played ; he did
not think she knew how to play, and he had
brought her to be taught by a companion.

As with strangers, with the distressed, with
children, so also he had deep sympathy with
the poor.   No man more cordially honoured
all to whom honour is due; but believing
that " God hath chosen the poor rich in faith,"
he did not quite approve of designating the
rich as " the better classes."   When he used
the expression he qualified it by saying " the
better classes, or rather the better-off classes."
His heart was singularly tender toward the

poor, and he had an open hand for their wants. Nothing touched him more than any case of suffering. He was easily imposed upon, but the imposition never soured him, and he was willing to submit to it for the chance of doing good. He said, "I find they know how to get round me; they say, 'You helped me before;' and I can never resist that; it teaches me how to pray,"—referring to the same plea so often used in the Psalms. He had a tender heart for every human being, and for every human want for this life and for the next. He would walk along the street with some poor man to whom he had given alms, and press upon him the greater gift of eternal life.

If he could resist the cry of no poor man, he could least of all resist a poor Jew; poverty and kindred to Jacob, combining in a double claim, came very close to his heart. The following is a single instance out of many. "One Friday evening in the year 1865 the Presbyterian city missionary of Montreal stepped into a store in Notre Dame Street owned by a Jew. He, and two of his fellow-countrymen who were present, seemed not unwilling to enter into conversation. One of the three knew the missionary, and introduced him to his friend the proprietor of the store. It was not long, however, ere the shopkeeper showed his Jewish leanings. He made the most furious attacks on Christianity and the New Testament, as well as on the English translation of the Bible. He produced a translation of the Old Testament, which he insisted was the only genuine translation. 'Suppose,' said the missionary to him, 'you were to have a Bible printed in Hebrew which would be a true translation of that vile and blasphemous production, and were to put that in the Synagogue instead of the authorized version of the Hebrew Scriptures, what would be done to you?' He looked amazed, and even scared. His two companions looked daggers at him; he seemed to wither in a moment under the keen glance of their eyes, which flashed with indignation. He laid aside his bravado, and, assuming a penitential look of shame and remorse, began this narrative:

" ' It is very wrong of me to speak to you and to malign your religion. I am now a rich man; but I was once poor. Some years ago I landed in Edinburgh without a penny; I had no friends. Walking along the street I saw an old man coming towards me with a kind face; I thought I would speak to him. He looked me kindly in the face, and asked me if I was a Jew; I said I was. He said, "Will you come home with me?" I said I would gladly do so, and I went home with him. He inquired very kindly into my history, and I told him all the truth. He kept me several weeks, and took a store for me, and gave me £30 to begin business. All his friends came round me, and I soon made a great deal of money. At length I could stand it no longer; it was all hypocrisy. I could not be a Christian; I could not give up my religion and my countrymen; I resolved I would fly from

Edinburgh. I put up a bit of paper in my window-shutter, with the words written on it : "Gone from home. Will be back in a few days." But I had come across the Atlantic, never more to visit Edinburgh. But I always think kindly of my benefactor, Dr. John Duncan, Professor of Hebrew in the Free Church College, Edinburgh. He was the greatest Hebrew scholar I ever met among the Gentiles, and a dear, good old man.' It was now near six o'clock in the evening, and the Jew hurried to put on his shutters ; so he hurried all three out into the street." [11]

But with all his liberality in giving, he never forgot that our first place and our chief exercise is to receive. "In the life of faith," he said, "distinguish between a taking faith and a giving faith. It is the want of the taking faith that causes the want of the giving faith. Let Christ have the greater blessedness of giving."

"The Song of the Shirt" laid hold on him, as Plato sometimes did, and with a firmer grasp. That startling sorrow touched the hearts of thousands, but stamped its image on his like a seal on softened wax, and the impression was seen on his face as if an affliction had visited his home. For weeks after its appearance the pitiful dirge seemed to engross his thoughts and affections. He referred to it from the pulpit, if my memory does not err, and was full of it in conversation. "'The Song of the Shirt,'" he said, "is one of the best sermons that has been preached for many a day. This lay sermon teaches a great lesson to the Church."

PLATO AND THE APOSTLE PAUL.

Plato, whom he called his "heathen theologian," was an object to him of admiration and love, and sometimes of excessive attraction. One week in particular he got absorbed in the Greek philosopher, who had quite the mastery over him, and seemed to take possession of all his faculties. It was in summer, when he had no external duties; and Plato held him fast, out of bed and in it, morning, noon, and night, through breakfast, dinner, and supper. Then conscience awoke; he saw that he had made Plato his idol for the time; he was thrown into darkness of spirit and weakness of body, and took longer to recover a good conscience towards God than he had taken to lose it. Men of impulsive and erratic intellect are usually on such terms with their consciences as easily to quiet its reproaches. But his conscience was sensitively, often morbidly, acute; and there was perhaps scarcely another man along with him in the world, who, with a conscience equally tender, was so apt to wound it, and was then so pained and cast down till the wound was healed.

But with all his admiration for Plato, he did not assign to him but to another the highest place among men of genius. "I look on the apostle Paul," he said, "as the greatest genius that ever lived."

MENTAL ABSENCE.

In his noted mental absence there was frequently an infantile simplicity that did not want its own charm. " Will you have another cup of tea, Mr. Duncan ?" said a lady to him with exemplary patience, after he had drained his cup fourteen times. " No, I thank you, madam," he replied; " I never take more than two cups of tea." This absence often showed itself by a forgetfulness of the presence of others, as if he had been alone. At dinner, in a company of ministers, following his constant habit of walking up and down when interested in a subject, he unconsciously rose and walked round the table, reasoning out his argument in his peripatetic course, till an elderly clergyman checked him a little sharply with the remark, " Sir, this cannot be allowed ; you are reasoning in a circle." The effect ascribed to the following incident must only have been for the moment, for he prayed long to recover a natural belief in the existence of matter. " He told me that among other curious conditions he was at one time a firm believer in Berkeleyism, immaterialism ; till one night groping, in the luxury of material and mental darkness, for his bed, his head came in smart contact with the bed-post, which knocked Berkeley out of it, leaving the bed-post mark." [10]

Sometimes, however, his absence of mind, with its forgetfulness of himself, showed itself also in a forgetfulness and disregard of the

feelings of others, for which no excuse can be
pleaded; which, if afterwards brought before
him, he would have been the first to condemn
as selfish; and which he was enabled in a
good measure to overcome in the later years of
his life. A startling and almost incredible instance of this thoughtlessness for himself and
others, at his second marriage, is graphically
described by his future son-in-law : "The day
he was to be married to Mrs. Torrance, he had
his niece in the house with him; the hour was
coming on, his niece sent him to his room to
dress. I suppose going to bed was in his mind
the sequence of undressing. However, the hour
of marriage came, and the cab to carry him;
no sign of the dressed bridegroom. His niece
went to see how it was, and found him in bed
sound asleep with a Hebrew book in his hand.
I was at the marriage, being a pupil of his; he
was deep in a Hebrew lesson with me in a
bay-window : the bride was brought in without
interrupting the lesson; some one came and
took him by the arm to lead him off to other
doings; his steps moved away, but his face remained turned to his scholar; his parting words
were, ' Well, mind we take that up another
time.'" [10]

His absences, on the other hand, were not
always untinged by consciousness; he could be
slyly absent when he did not care to be present. There was a true knowledge of self,
as well as an acknowledgment of self-indul-
gence, in the following confession of "lazi-
ness;" which he knew to be a besetting sin, not

intellectually but practically, and which sometimes half-consciously put on the cloak of absence. One morning he came in to us of his
own accord, all ready to start by an early train
from Pesth, and I said to him, "How is it
that you are so often first? People at home
think you are not able to look after yourself."
He replied, "I'm lazy, and they think I'm
stupid; at home I know I'll be looked after."

With all his practical absence of mind he
had a singular presence of mind intellectually.
A friend says of him most justly : "He had a
wonderful power of knowing exactly what one
meant. I don't think his mind ever wandered
if he were speaking of what either interested
you or himself, only from conversational tattle."
He had not only plenty of mind to fall back
upon, but he had it thoroughly and immediately at command. If he was attending to
what was said, his wits were never to seek for
uttering apt thought upon it. Some one mistaking for Scripture a beautiful sentiment
drawn from a very different source, asked him,
Where is that text in the Bible, "He tempers
the wind to the shorn lamb?" He returned
the doubly unlooked-for answer, "That could
not be in the Bible, for it is not true." This
combination of quickness and fulness of reply
was not by an occasional sally of intellect, but
his daily habit of speech.

Notwithstanding his often excessive want of
observation of outward objects, he could observe
acutely when he directed his attention. "I
used," he said, "to think of Samson as a giant;

but I was struck with a painting in which his hand was smaller than that of Delilah on whose lap it lay. This picture suggested to me that the Bible speaks of his strength as entirely miraculous in connexion with his Nazarite locks; and that there is no reason to think that he was naturally larger than other men."

His disregard of the forms of society, which was extreme and to some persons intolerable, had its counterpart in an exquisite refinement of sentiment. He had a high esteem for taste, and for politeness in its inner beauty. He felt and often expressed a keen dislike of all that was " vulgar ;" this was a term of condemnation which he often used, but always applying it to the real man and not to his outer coating, whether coarse or fine. In all that was truly refined, in character, in word, in act, he found a strong attraction.

INCIDENTS IN TRAVELLING.

In his first journey to Pesth he was the subject of an amusing mistake at Cologne. " Our names," says his son-in-law, " had to be entered in a book at the hotel. In his Puritanic severity the doctor wrote : John Duncan, minister, and wife, Annabella Torrance and Annie, R. Smith, and W. Allan. Next morning we had the honour of reading that there had arrived at the hotel : John Duncan, one of Her Britannic Majesty's ministers, Lady Torrance and family, Gentlemen Smith and Allan."

In 1862 I was appointed with Dr. Duncan to visit our mission at Pesth. Dr. Craig of Hamburgh conducted him to Prague, where he was left two days, while I went with my son to Breslau, to join him again at Vienna. If we had parted for a year, he could not have been more relieved and glad to meet us. His joy was partly for the opportunity of pouring out his pent-up thoughts, for which he had found no listener for two days ; for when he was not absorbed, an incessant stream of talk kept flowing from him whenever and wherever there was an ear either to welcome or to submit. In travelling he would talk all day or all night without intermission ; and it was no light penance for him to have had his mouth helplessly shut during a long journey for want of a listener. But his delight in meeting us was still greater, because during our absence he had been reduced to a state of hunger from inability to order what he wanted, or to know what to order. The want of the practical extended even to language ; and the only foreign tongue we heard him speak was Latin, which he spoke fluently and with great beauty, and in which he was familiar with the shades of pronunciation in various countries. His minute knowledge of the structure of many languages, of their exact pronunciation and their peculiar idioms, was of no service to himself or to others in communicating the common wants of a traveller, or in translating these out of English at the moment. He said himself that the only languages he spoke with ease were English and Latin. But when he was left alone at Prague he had not only the difficulty of expressing his wants, but of knowing what to want. The result was that he could order nothing eatable, and lived, I believe, on little besides coffee and its accompaniments for two days. When we met again, and reached Vienna, he was asked what he would have for dinner. That was too hard a question for him, but he answered, " Let us have a good dinner ; our life in this world is drawing to an end ; let us enjoy it while it lasts." The idea was the opposite of the Epicurean one ; it did not regard this life as the portion of man, but only as a brief yet not despicable part of his entire existence.

But while he did not despise the good gifts of God, no discomfort would induce him to eat " of things strangled and of blood." One day he came late to dinner at a friend's house, with the breath frozen on his whiskers and beard, and a smoking plate of hare soup was set before him ; but he pushed it back muttering, " Blood ! take it away." The incident disconcerted him ; he was dull all the evening, and wished to go away early, but was prevailed upon to stay and take the family prayers. He relieved his conscience by reading the chapter in Isaiah which contains the passage, " Broth of abominable things is in their vessels." Then the cloud cleared away, and he remained till twelve or one o'clock in the highest spirits, and speaking most interestingly, discussing poetry and all the poets, walking up and down the room, and only stopping to ask, "What? what?" as he used to do when he wanted some response.

LIKING FOR ANECDOTE.

He was fond of anecdote, but it was always of such a kind as to illustrate his point most aptly; and any anecdote that illustrated character had a special attraction for him. He repeated the following story about a Jew in Hungary with great zest, because it brought out two characteristic but hardly congruous features of the nation—"The Jews are very kind to the poor of their own nation, but their love of money still comes out through their charity. A rich and benevolent Jewish banker called on a widow lady who had been left in poor circumstances. After kindly condoling with her on her bereavement, he presented her with a bill for £500. He was a Jew, and had a generous heart to a sister in sorrow; but he was a Jewish banker, and could not miss the chance of doing a little stroke of business in giving his alms; and so he said before leaving, 'Now, madam, you will have to get that bill exchanged, and if you will employ me, I will do it for you as cheap as any one else.'"

Our mutual Recognition in the future state he never doubted; but the only way in which he illustrated it was by an anecdote which he was fond of repeating :—"A pious old couple had been talking of the joys of heaven, and Janet said to her husband, 'Do you think,

John, we'll know one another in heaven?'
John paused, laid down his pipe, and asked in
his turn, 'Do you think, Janet, we'll be greater
fools there than we are here?'" He never
cared to say any more on the subject; this
reply always appeared to him to settle the
whole question.

The following warning against a subtle form
of Antinomianism he repeated with the force
with which he dealt all his blows against that
error :—" A minister of the gospel" (who lived,
I think, in Wales), "had a godly woman in his
congregation who was often in such distress of
soul that she could do nothing but read and
pray, to the neglect of household duties. The
good man said much to comfort her, but it was
all in vain. At last one day coming to the
house, and finding her as usual poring over
the Bible, he walked up to her and called out
sternly, 'Is there no fear of God in this
house?'"

On Philosophy he said — " I am of the
mind of the countryman who in arguing with
a lawyer, whatever the point in dispute, ap-
pealed to the Bible. Said the lawyer, 'But
there are many things in the Bible against
Philosophy.' 'The waur then for Philosophy,'
said the countryman."

The exaltation of Faith out of its own place
of a handmaid awakened his jealousy. He
said that "Some men's Trinity consisted of the
Father, and the Son, and Faith ;" and he frequently repeated the following anecdote, with
the names and circumstances. "At a High-

land communion in a meeting for ' speaking to the question,' on a Friday evening, the subject selected was Faith. One after another of the ' men' spoke in glowing terms of the power and the triumphs of Faith, and each speaker exalted it more than the one before him. At last their esteemed minister, jealous for the honour of the Lord Jesus Christ, stood up and said, ' I ask, Was Faith crucified for you ; or were ye baptized in the name of Faith ?'"

LETTERS.

His letters are a wonderful transcript of himself, full of the deepest religious thought and experience, and the warmest affection, mingled with theology and languages. " Many thanks to William for his beautiful Koran ; it is one of the finest MSS. I have ever seen.—My deep conviction is that the presence of God is very remark*ably*, but very little remark*edly*, with us.—Tell dear Nabby to make sure work of her thorough conversion to God.—Describe to me, as far as possible, the sounds of the following Arabic letters (naming six letters). Do you sound the last as the Italian *a*, or with the bleating sound between *a* and η ? Is the previous letter sounded as *i*, or, as it is by the Persians, *e* ?—Nabby, lassie, and your wee lassies, how much I long to see you, and what a pained heart I have every time I read your entreaties to come. Cheer up, my bird, your place, though trying, is a deeply important one ; the Lord may yet suffer us to meet sooner than we expect. Do you ever tell the darlings stories about queer old grandpapa? What lingo do they speak? Polyglott I suppose. Has that nasty trick left you, my bird?"

Out of more than twenty letters, from some of which extracts have already been given, we have selected three, not like the others in variety, but less peculiarly private. The first is addressed to a respected elder of the Church, in acknowledgment of a present made to him, as one of those who in the Disruption of the Church of Scotland sacrificed their position for conscience' sake.

"EDINBURGH, 21*st May* 1844.

"MY DEAR SIR,—Though I feel deeply your kindness, yet I might have contented myself, in the present pressure and hurry, with cherishing the feeling in my heart without expressing it; but Mrs. D. will not allow me. 'You must write,' she says, 'for I never felt so *conceity* of any present.' I do thank you, sir, more heartily than if *personal* friendship had dictated the gift, for the Free Church is dearer to me than myself. But I trust that, though you modestly mention only the Free Church, the real motive is *love* to one higher far than any portion of the Church or even the whole Church, even Him 'who loved the Church and gave himself for it.' I hope it has been given to a disciple—*that* I hope for myself, in the name of a disciple—*that* I fondly hope for you.

"But, my dear sir, we must first give *ourselves*

to Christ before He will accept anything else from us. I trust you have done so. If not, do it without delay ; if you have, do it again, and do it more fully. But *something* goes *before* that ; we must first receive *Him.* By God's grace we do not give ourselves to Christ and receive him ; but receive Him and give ourselves to him. Ay, *something* goes even before that : *He* apprehends *us,* whereupon we follow on, if we may apprehend that for which we are apprehended of Christ Jesus. 1*st,* Christ apprehends us : 2*d,* we receive him : 3*d,* we give *ourselves* to him : 4*th,* we give *ours,* both the *dispensed* and the *retained,* to Him.

"Again I thank you. If you have given aught to him, He will not only thank but reward you with the reward—*Oh* mark and mind this!—not of merit but of grace.—Yours in the Gospel of the Lord Jesus,

"JOHN DUNCAN." [16]

The next, a few years later, is addressed to his step-daughter, Mrs. Allan :—

"EDINBURGH, *Monday,* 17 *Jay.* /48.

"MY DEARLY BELOVED DAUGHTER,—The painful news of your severe illness has deeply, deeply wounded my heart. I grieve to think how little I did for your good, and how much to grieve you, when the Lord gave me the sadly neglected opportunity of being with you in that distant land. Oh that I had better learned to count all things but loss for the excellency of the knowledge of Christ Jesus, my Lord !

But though *I* neglected, thanks be to Him who neglected not, but remembering came to fulfil his holy promise, 'I will be as the dew unto Israel;' and who in the time of visitation left not *your own* soul to be as the heath in the wilderness, which knoweth not when good cometh. The sight, yea, even the remembrance, of a father's smile, helps much to bear aright a father's rod. Such close and tender ties bind us together, that in chastening you He scourgeth us. But we desire through grace to remember, what we are so prone to forget, 'The exhortation which speaketh unto us as unto children,' Hebrews xii. 5, 6, with the sweet exposition and application, verses 7, 8, 9, 10. *I*, saith our blessed Lord, am the vine, *ye* are the branches (John xv. 5), *my Father* is the husbandman (ver. 1); every branch in me that beareth not fruit he taketh away, and every branch that beareth fruit, he purgeth it, that it may bring forth more fruit. Our souls, weak and conscious of sin, tremble, it is true, at the merest glimpse of the sharp pruning-hook; and sure that we have been but little, alarmed lest we may not have been at all, fruitful, we feel the overpowering awfulness of the words 'he taketh away.' Still we would not shun the truth, the most searching and most dreadful of the truths of God. We would not have it otherwise. We should not, must not, will not, can not, be satisfied with a dead, unreceptive, unfruitful connexion with Christ—the baptism of water and its concomitants, without the renewing of the Holy Ghost.

We have, I trust, been put under this sharp stroke of the knife : being by the iron entering our very souls cut off not only from legal hope and dead works, but from carnal gospellizing and dead faith of our own formation (Epistle of James); which pleased us when we had a form of godliness, but denied, at least practically and in heart, the power. Blessed taking away, which terminates not in apostasy in time, or rejection at death, but is followed by the Husbandman's engrafting into union, spiritual, internal, vital, receptive of fatness, and productive of fruit. Then, though the fruit be but scanty and immature, and though nature and carnality tremble and shrink, the spirit born of Spirit welcomes gratefully, ay, and gladly, the sharpest instrument which purges to bring forth more fruit. The Husbandman, I think, hope, trust, believe, has been finding some fruit among you, and in you. The pruning-knife might and should have been expected. But, alas ! how foolish are we, and how slow of heart to learn 'the way of JEHOVAH, and the judgment of *our God*' (Jer. v. 4).

" This, I hope, may find you much recovered, brought back from the gates of death to praise the LORD in the gates of the daughter of Zion. If so, ponder well, dear child, that word ' afterwards,' Hebrews xii. 11. Yet fear will intrude. Richard Cameron, when the dragoons of Charles II. were closing on the heaven-canopied assembly met to worship Him for whose sake they were killed all the day and counted as sheep for the slaughter, prayed :

I

' Lord, spare the green, and take the ripe !'
But it becomes not us to seek to dictate to
infinite goodness, acting sovereignly in infinite
wisdom. He *may* do what He *will* with *his
own.* Only He *does* not, *cannot* WILL, but
according to His own faithful promise and
loving heart. *He* cannot hurt the sheep, who
' loved them and gave Himself for them.' But
the application in fulfilment to individuals of
those distinct petitions of his prayer,—' Holy
Father, I pray not that Thou shouldest take
them out of the world, but that Thou shouldest
keep them from the evil,' and 'Father, I will
that *they* also whom *Thou* hast given *me* be
with me where I am, that *they* may behold *my*
glory which *Thou* hast given *me*,'—lies between
Him and the *Father*, who hath ' put the times
and the seasons in his own power.' (*I, Thou,
they,* what pronouns, significant of what persons, and joined in what relations !)

" How sweet is the 23d Psalm : you will
stop here, and read it, or hear it read.

" To that Shepherd and Bishop of souls,
with mingled and accordant grief and joy, I
commit you, my dear, dear daughter, in life
and in death. May He receive you ! He will.
Come to Him, come again, come closer, embrace, cleave with purpose of heart. I am
persuaded : Rom. viii. 38.

" Such are the heart's desires and prayers,
such the hopes, and such the trust Godward
concerning you of your earthly father,

                 " JOHN DUNCAN."

The third letter is dated nearly twenty years later, and is addressed to two young men laid aside by illness, one of whom was taken by the Lord, and the other left :—

"Augt. 3*d,* 1866.

" MY VERY DEAR YOUTHS,—To what blessed use grace turns those things, bitter in themselves, because the fruit of sin,—afflictions, distresses, even death. I trust you are led to unite the feeling of affliction with humbling sense of sin, *light* affliction with *heavy* sin. I hope that the Lord hath taught you in some good measure that, young as you are, and privileged as you have been, *sin hath abounded ;* so abounded as that your case were utterly hopeless on any other ground than the revealed harmony of the divine perfections, God in Christ, well pleased for His righteousness' sake, shining forth with benignant aspect, and drawing attraction to the sinful children of Adam, and rejoicing with *singing* (Zeph. iii. 17) over every soul which would gladly just let the grace of God, the God of grace, have the glory, *all* the glory of its salvation.

Gethsemane (Luke xxii. 40-46). } Doctrine
Calvary (xxiii. ; Rom. iii. 9-31). } of grace.

ἰλαστήριον, Propitiatory, mercy-seat. } Exercise.
Psa. xxxv., xxxix. ; Isa. xxxviii. }

Rom. xiv. 7-9. Resignation. The receiving and resting on and in Christ, and so leaving life and death to the disposal of Him whose we are ; trusting to his grace, if we live, to enable us to live to Him, and resolving in the

strength of promised grace so to live ; and if
we die, why, then—' Whether we live, we live
unto the Lord ; and whether we die, we die
unto the Lord : whether we live, therefore, or
die, we are the Lord's.'

"I leave this because I feel I am only
muddling the clear water with my feet. May
the Lord himself apply these words of grace to
us all, young and old. Sure I am that thus
they shall be a staff through the laborious
journey of life, and a soft pillow on which to
repose our dying heads. I fear that I have
loaded you with too much. Your dear father,
as a faithful under-shepherd, will guide your
exercise, giving you your portion of meat in
due season.

" The Lord bless you, my dear boys. And
may it please Him to spare you, raise you up,
and send you forth, with the sweet odour of
sanctified affliction, for the gracious end which
the Psalmist had in view. Psalm ix. 13, 14.
Pray for me. The Lord is specially near to
his people in affliction. When He comes near,
O speak a word for me ! I deeply feel that I
need it. I trust I would greatly value it.—
With much love, yours,   JOHN DUNCAN.

" Looking unto Jesus. A large field, a little
as you are able. Not slothful, not precipitate.
He *waits* to be gracious ; ' Blessed are they
who *wait* for Him.' "

DEJECTION.

Spiritual depression was a frequently recurring element in Dr. Duncan's life, which he could have concealed more than he did, but took no pains to cover, and could not really have hid by any effort. He was very impulsive and very transparent ; did little to repress his emotions, and nothing to disguise them. Impulsiveness, however, did not bear in him its too natural fruit of changeableness in his opinions or in his friendships, in both of which he was steadfast and constant. " The Lord hateth putting away," was a very favourite Bible saying of his for the constancy of the love of God, and he sought to follow it. But his feelings were strong, and carried him away, and he cared too little to keep them to himself ; minding more the reality of things than their appearance.

Emotions of spiritual joy did not come out in him by speaking of himself or of his own feelings ; but either in the pulpit or in social intercourse, it was by magnifying Jesus Christ, by an evident rejoicing in the Lord that could not be hid, and an exultant unfolding of his beauty. It was otherwise with his spiritual sorrow ; yet it would be unjust to assign as the simple cause of the difference, that the sorrow exceeded the joy, although it often presented this aspect. If the one was not the true measure of the other, yet the depth and duration of his sorrow arose from the hiding of the face of that King in his beauty, in whom he had " rejoiced with joy unspeakable, and full of glory." In answer to representations of God's goodness and redeeming power he would reply, " Oh, I know that his hand is not shortened that it cannot save, nor his ear heavy that it cannot hear, but my sins have hid his face from me."

His complaint was the echo of Job's : " Oh that I knew where I might find him," and his distress so absorbing and so restless that he could not refrain from uttering, and even publishing it. In his continual claim and charge, " Pray for me," it came out like the charge to the daughters of Jerusalem : " If ye find my Beloved, tell him that I am sick of love "—

> " To those who fear the Lord, I speak,
>   Is my Beloved near ?
>   The Bridegroom of my soul I seek ;
>   Oh, when shall He appear ?"

In his distance and desire for restored nearness he spoke of his desolation to all whom he met ; to his friends, to his students, to strangers. His sorrow was deep, and its utterance was extreme ; yet in spreading it abroad his course was not essentially different from that of the Bride in the mystic song, and its burden was entirely the same as hers : " My Beloved hath withdrawn himself, and is gone : I sought him, but I could not find him ; I called him, but he gave me no answer."

In his self-jealousy he departed from the simplicity of Christ, and darkened and weakened himself by a fruitless self-inspection ; but he knew well what he wanted to recover. He

was tenderly alive to the gracious affections
that are inseparable from true believing in
Christ, and he would not be satisfied with the
coldness of death under the name of life. He
insisted, " Let no man take for granted that
he has grace irrespective of the exercise of
gracious affections." He recollected his own
intense earnestness at the first, his childlike
helplessness, and how he counted all things
loss for the excellency of the knowledge of
Christ ; he " remembered how he had received
and heard," and he desired to " hold fast and
repent." This life-long warning, which he gave
both by word and by his own example against
what he looked upon as an antinomian security
and a false ease in Zion, was made available
by the Spirit to " the profit of many that they
might be saved."

An extreme searching into the roots of
things, and an excessive self-scrutiny, often
threw him into dejection, and into seeming,
though not always into real, despondency. Out
of this state a word in season would sometimes
help him, but for the most part it seemed to
take its course before he was relieved. After
reasoning long with him, and trying many
arguments to answer his objections against
himself, and remove his fears, he would reply
at last—" You don't know how I have sinned ;
there's no good in polluting my lips by con-
fessing it to man."

Much as he doubted his salvation, he did
not conclude positively that he was uncon-
verted, far less that he was incapable of salva-

tion. In his low states he did not like to speak
of his conversion ; but when he did speak of it
at other times, it was usually as a grand work
of God and of redemption. It was sin after
conversion that troubled and burdened him ;
rather it was recent sin, or present sinfulness
and distance from God. His belief in the per-
severance of the saints might have enabled him
to argue his saintship from his conversion ; yet
that helped him little, because he held strongly
that the saintship must be proved by the per-
severance.

But that wherein he most wronged his own
soul was in his excessive refusal of the consolation which he would himself have offered to
every sinner outside the kingdom. " If any
man on the street, whatever his sins might
have been, were to ask you whether Christ
would receive him if he came to Him, would
you not confidently assure him, He will in no
wise cast you out ?" "Certainly ; but that
gives me no relief." " Were your state as
desperate as that of the thief on the cross, and
your death as near, would not Jesus receive
you ?" "Yes ; but his case does not meet
mine." He would add, "I have not come to
the conviction that He will not save me ; I
believe that He is able, and I have not concluded that he is unwilling." He felt, as all
God's children do, the exceeding aggravation
of sin after having "tasted that the Lord is
gracious ;" he would take no comfort from the
fact that in that case there must have been
grace toward himself to be sinned against ;

and he found himself in some respects at a greater distance from Christ than even the children of this world. He would conclude by saying, " I can get no deliverance except by acquiescing in the justice of God in my reprobation."

The difficulty of explaining how recovery out of darkness was harder for him than for other children of God, may be partly met by one of his own solutions. " I am naturally of a sceptical turn of mind, and since I have been delivered from doubt about God and the great truths of redemption, my scepticism has taken the form of doubt about my own salvation." Occasionally he was free from these depressions for a considerable period ; but for the forty years during which I knew him he was subject to them, although they were less frequent and less severe in his latter years. But his dejection was seldom if ever so great as to render him unable or unwilling to comfort others in distress ; and when his own prayers for himself have been most plaintive and desponding, he would, if requested, give thanks for another in words and tones of gracious elevation and dignity.

His depression was due to various causes, some evident, others latent. " He that increaseth knowledge, increaseth sorrow," was true of him in the abundance of both ; and if his knowledge had been narrower, his suffering would have been lighter. He could walk further into the sea than other men without losing his feet; but then he was tempted to wade beyond his own depth, and sunk into a sea of sorrow whence he found it hard to reach the shore again.

The wise man's warning, "My son, be admonished, of making many books there is no end," he took by the forelock and made no beginning. But the second clause of this admonition, "Much study is a weariness of the flesh," came more home to him than to the most voluminous authors. He seemed, indeed, to be equal to an amount of mental fatigue and of bodily neglect which very few could have stood ; but there can be no doubt that much of his spiritual darkness was the inevitable fruit of the mental exhaustion which was the result of his excessive study.

The cause of darkness, however, which was most obvious to himself, and which sometimes sprang from a very definite origin, was a wounded conscience. His restless intellect was a frequent snare ; and also his want of order and regularity, and of submission to every-day system in common duties, in which there is often so little life, but on which both the fruit and the very root of life so largely depend.

" I am deficient in order," was his own confession, " it is sinful ; we must remember that God is a God of order." [4] But the seductive fruit of "the tree of knowledge" often tempted him, to the wounding of his conscience and the death of his peace. He would allow himself to be engrossed with books for days, till his heart smote him for the little time and thought given to higher objects. " He said that his excessive fondness for linguistic studies caused him to forget himself, and then ' God came upon him with a vengeance, and awoke him.' " [4]

In one of his forlorn states, which had lasted for weeks, he said to a friend who called on him : " I have been making idols of languages, and God is now saying to me, ' These are thy gods, and as thou hast forsaken me, I will forsake thee.' " " But Christ hath redeemed us from the curse of the law." " Yes, the curse causeless shall not come, and it has come upon me." " Doctor, one of the brethren told us lately that when he was a student in the Hebrew class, the Professor came to the class one morning in a very low state of mind, which lasted for a considerable time while he prayed ; but before the prayer was finished, the clouds seemed to roll away, and as soon as it was over he cried out : ' Dear young gentlemen, I have had a glimpse of Jesus.' Do you remember anything of that ? " He had stood looking at his friend and stroking his beard, then shook his head and started off; but he immediately turned back and clapping him on the shoulder said : " That's what I want, that's what I want ; thank you for that word." In an instant the load was gone ; he sat down and spoke first of union with Christ, and then asked many questions about the Welsh language, and he appeared in church next Sabbath well and happy.[3]

" In another of his low moods," writes one of our ministers, " he called on the Rev. John Walker of Perth, whose views of grace have

always been singularly clear.   He began: ' Mr.
Walker, I 'm thinking of going back to the law
again.'   ' I have no objection to your going
back to the law, if you go to it as David went,
" For the commandments of *my* God I purpose
to obey ;" I have no objection to your going as
David did.   What, after the law has been our
schoolmaster to bring us unto Christ, go back
again to be lashed by the schoolmaster ?'
' You 're quite right, Mr. Walker, you 're quite
right.'   Long after, when I met Dr. Duncan in
Edinburgh, he said to me,—' You have a minister in Perth, a man of some peculiarities, but
withal a superior divine, and a good and sound
spiritual casuist ?'   ' Oh, that will be Mr.
Walker you mean ?'   ' Yes, Walker, Walker ;
well, you know, I liked Walker ; yes, I liked
Walker.'   When once in spiritual darkness
myself, and darkness from perplexing providen-
tial circumstances, walking home from church
with Dr. Duncan one day, I mentioned
generally my state to him.   He said several
things, and at parting said this,—' Well, the
Lord turns the darkness into light ; and it is
not merely that He brings light after the
darkness, but the darkness itself he makes
into light.' " [15]

The following is a striking but severe description of the impulsive source of his depression :   " He comes into some new, impelling
sphere.   At first the subjects proper to the
occasion engage his whole heart, mind, impulses ;
they are new, fresh, interesting ; they have not
settled down into the distasteful drudgery of

duty, or been replaced by some new attraction.
And now the man is at his best, and a wonderful best it is. Those were great times in Pesth,
glad times, healthy times, while Dr. Duncan
continued at the work, while his impulses, his
inclinations coincided with his duties, or were
kept in subordination to them. But there lay
his weakness; he had in this direction no self-
control. He threw himself with his usual
abandonment, his disregard of every consideration and claim, into the study of the Magyar;
and his conduct in the matter of that language
has been repeated every time he has come into
similar circumstances. He prosecutes the study,
doing violence to the ordinary rules of health,
in food, drink, and rest; the books are at the
table, in the closet, in the bed; religious exercises omitted or distasteful; the good, the
convenience of others forgotten as much as his
own. Is it anything unnatural that there
should come a break-down; a break-down of
body, mind, conscience, spirit, self-respect, confidence toward God?" [10]

But it must be taken into account that the
nearly uncontrollable temper of his mind was
to take everything in long stretches, language,
philosophy, religion itself; and religion was
thus apt to be cast down for a time from its
supreme throne. But religion was not only
much, but infinitely more to him than philosophy or language; he entered into it with an
impulse, an entireness, a self-abandonment, of
which few men are capable. More than in
philosophy or in languages, he excelled other

men in religion; not in the knowledge of its doctrines only, but in its practical possession of his heart, in the fear of God, in devotion to Jesus Christ, in love to men.

Over against this account of defect we must set his own penitent confession of it in a similar instance at a later period. " I have often thought with grief and shame on the inconsistency of my conduct when with you, and on the offence which it was calculated to give. I came out with, as I supposed—and cannot yet say but that it was indeed in some measure—a desire to promote God's glory, and to labour in the vineyard. But I did not duly watch and pray, but yielded to the temptation of my idol *linguistics*, the well-stored library presenting so favourable an opportunity. And so my heart wickedly was withdrawn from God, prayer much restrained, and my trust and hope much more hypocritical than I then knew, though I could not but have a lurking suspicion. To you I must have been a great *stumbling-block*, and—for I know your affection—a *grief*. Blessed be the Lord, He hath sharply rebuked me, and set my sin in this, and more than this —oh how much ! what mountains, what mountains !—before mine eyes. Still He says ' Return,' and permits the prayer ' Draw me.' Still I am· permitted and commanded to look toward His holy temple, to the mercy-seat, and to the Mediator of the new covenant who hath entered in with His own blood, having obtained eternal redemption. The residue of the Spirit is with Him. He is waiting to be gracious,

and His precious blood sprinkled on the conscience by the Holy Spirit purgeth from all
sin. I have been far too selfish, confined,
miserably lacking in diffusive affection. Pity
me, pray for me. Let us love one another for
Christ's sake, though I be so unworthy."

"Now, Dr. Duncan, you are getting off the
Centre," Miss Sandeman would say to him,
when she saw him beginning to be absorbed in
study. "Not far," he replied at the moment;
but after a few days he would say with sorrow, "I wish I had listened to you in time."

He by no means held, however, that the
recovery of a believer is of necessity slow, and
gave in his own experience this example of
instant restoration :—"I remember one occasion of having been overtaken by sin, and I
abhorred myself; but I found immediate forgiveness, and was in a moment filled with the
love of God and with joy in the Holy Ghost."

Notwithstanding his depressions about his
own spiritual state, his mind otherwise and as
a whole was singularly free from any morbid
taint. The general cast of his thoughts and
views was bright, and the tone of his feelings
cheerful with the glow of mental and spiritual
health.

VIVID HOPE OF THE LIFE TO COME.

His frequent darkness did not debar him
from brighter thoughts of Jesus Christ than
belong to most who are strangers to it. In
one of these sad states, after he had spoken in

his own wondrous way about Jesus Christ, I said to him, " You could not have such thoughts of Christ, except God had taught you." He replied, "That's just what puts me wrong; as long as I am thinking of Christ I'm happy; and if my friends would just let me a-be [alone], I would be all right. But when they hear me speak of the beauty of Jesus Christ they say : ' Then you'll be going to heaven;' and that makes me ask if I am fit for heaven, and I get all dark." At another time, when I asked him to prèach for me, he answered, " I'll be glad to preach, if you'll take the prayers; I'm not able to pray at present, but I can preach a bit, and would like it;" and it was frequently at such seasons that his preaching was eminently beautiful. He knew well what it is to " rejoice in Christ Jesus;" but he said, "Spiritual joy is a delicate thing; it is easily spoiled; it requires much tenderness."

At a Communion season, two or three years before his death, he was intending to preach on the connexion between the sixth and seventh chapters of the Romans, and had laboured hard for several days in a very great but deep cogitation, into which few of his hearers could have followed him. Happily one of the other ministers took his text, and he felt that he must give up his subject, although it had not been handled. When once he was fairly unhooked from a weight of thought, lying at too great a depth for himself to reach without a severe mental strain, he rose buoyantly to the open sunlight on the surface of the dark waters.

From the deepest subtlety he passed immediately into the most perfect simplicity; with thoughts clear and attractive to a child, but of great value as well as exquisite beauty; as if he had brought up with him from the deep pearls for which he was not searching.

That evening he gave out for his text, " In my Father's house are many mansions : if it were not so, I would have told you. I go to prepare a place for you;" and transferred his hearers into the heart of those mansions by investing them with an individuality and a brightness beside which the tawdry, and what he would have called the " vulgar," descriptions of heaven which are sometimes thrust on us were vague and colourless ; yet with a strictness of adherence to scriptural truth that made the footing sensibly firm. Far more than other men on earth, he appeared to be at home in those many mansions in the great palace above. This promise of many abodes in the one great home of the Father, he held to be distinct from the more general promise of the kingdom prepared for the redeemed from before the foundation of the world, and to denote a special preparation for each by Christ after his ascension. It therefore went on simultaneously with the spiritual progress of the individual believer, and was a preparation of his mansion in heaven according to the progressive preparation of himself on earth ; so that the present state of his heavenly mansion was indicated by his present spiritual condition, his personal

K

preparation here securing its corresponding preparation above. There was thus a perfect fitness between each of the redeemed and his own special abode in the King's palace; he being fitted for it, and it fitted for him.

Yet he saw more than he was able to describe; and the elevation and intense energy of his spirit helped his hearers upward towards his own high position, and aided them to see what he was contemplating; so that his mere words, even if exactly written, could not but fail to exhibit the bright heavenly scene which he sought to portray. At the same time his wonted wisdom and care were brought out in reply to the question, "But why did you read and repeat without a syllable of comment the words in the middle of your text, 'If it were not so, I would have told you'?" "Because I am not sure that I see their meaning; I have sometimes thought I had got it, but I can't make it out."

Of the future glory he said, on another occasion, "There are things unseen and eternal, and there are men and women looking at them, who under the light of them, brighter than ten thousand stars, are marching on through afflictions, trials, temptations, unto them. There is a land of holiness, of peace, of joy, of love. There, the Holy Ghost filling every soul born of him and nourished of him, the spirit born of the Spirit basks eternally in the contemplation of the Divine glory and excellence and love."

He cherished a constant impression of the perfect adaptation of the Word of God for the life that now is; this was a favourite subject with him in speaking of the unity of the Bible, as embracing both the Old and New Testaments. But the present visible world was to him in close connexion with the world unseen; and not merely with the care of Divine providence, but with the ministration of angels. He did not, indeed, like one of the American divines of last century, whose conscience chid him for his forgetfulness of the angels, set apart an entire day to meditate on those spirits of light. But they formed a frequent subject of thought and conversation; he liked to speak of what he believed to be angelic interpositions in the case of his own family; and his manner of noticing them brought out his own practical hope of heaven. He would sometimes ask, " Who is your favourite angel? which of them would you like best to see? Many would choose Gabriel; but the one I most desire to see is the angel who came down to strengthen my Lord in his agony in the garden." In his contemplation of angels, as in all things else, his mind returned instinctively to his Lord Jesus Christ as its attractive loadstone, and specially to Jesus Christ in his death, or in Bible words, which he often quoted, to " Christ crucified in weakness."

DOMESTIC EVENTS.

In his domestic history Dr. Duncan met with an irreparable bereavement nine years after his return to Scotland, in the loss of his

wife, who died in 1852. She entered zealously
and intelligently into all his work, and was
beloved and highly esteemed in the Mission at
Pesth ; and she was of the greatest service to
him in every way while she was spared to be
with him in Edinburgh. He often spoke of
divine help which they had enjoyed together
during her life, even what he regarded as
angelic interposition ; and he repeated two
texts brought home to him on the day of her
funeral : one for her, " He that believeth in
me, though he were dead, yet shall he live ;"
and another for himself, " And whosoever
liveth and believeth in me shall never die."
She left an only daughter, now for a number
of years married to the Rev. Adolph Spaeth,
a respected minister of the German Church in
Philadelphia.

After her death Dr. Duncan asked Miss
Mary Sandeman of Perth, an intimate friend
of his late wife, to take charge of his house ; a
lady remarkably suited for the rather difficult
duty. The fitness consisted not in resemblance
to him but rather in contrast, except that she
shared abundantly in that grace of which he
was a partaker. Of a cheerful disposition and
sunny countenance, the joy of the Lord was
peculiarly her strength. Into his personal
doubts and the specialties of his thoughts she
did not care to enter ; but she had a clear and
acute mind, was highly intelligent in divine
truth, and taught with great success large
Bible classes of young ladies. Her presence in
the house must often have been a great rest

and repose to his mind; and the tenderness was most touching with which he watched over her dying hours. For some time before her death she was unable to speak, and he thought her scarcely able to listen. In visiting her he asked me first to repeat a single text to her, and then to pray in another room, himself walking into her room with wonderful softness and care. Beyond his expectation, though quite unable to utter a word, when I repeated a text she raised her eyes fully to heaven with a smile of singular sweetness; looking brightly to where her anchor was fixed within the veil, and evidently desiring to hear more of that Word which had been her food through life, and was now her support and her joy in death. She died in 1869, after residing with Dr. Duncan for seventeen years. In her charge she was succeeded by my friend Miss Marianne Robertson, daughter of the late Dr. Robertson, minister of the parish of Cambuslang. Having been for many years a member of Free St. Luke's Church, of which Dr. Duncan was an elder, intimately acquainted with him personally, and with his thoughts doctrinal and experimental, and accustomed to write his sermons and communion addresses, Miss Robertson was well qualified to take those notes of his conversation that form so valuable a portion of the materials with which Dr. Brown has been supplied for his biography.

THE END.

Dr. Duncan died in his 75th year, after a few weeks' illness, on the 26th of February 1870. One Sabbath evening, three years before his death, he broke out into this soliloquy : "There are heaps o' things in the past, mercies, sins, forgivenesses ; in seventy years and better there is a great deal to look back to. Alas! I have never done a sinless action during it all ; I have never done a sinless action during the seventy years. I don't say but by God's grace there may have been some holy action done, but never a sinless action during the seventy years. What an awful thing is human life ! and what a solemn consideration it should be to us, that we have never done a sinless action all our life, that we have never done one act that did not need to be pardoned." He added afterwards, with singular self-knowledge, but with a judgment of himself too severe to be just : "Ohone ! Ohone! I wish I had a little more personal faith. I think with the Psalmist that these things are more precious than gold, yea, than much fine gold ; but I cannot go so well with him in that, that ' they are sweeter also than honey and the honeycomb.' I stick at that ; that has been often a plague with me ; the precious things were more as casketed jewels than as meat and drink. They delight the intellect; but oh, I wish I had a loving heart ! I go mourning all the day for want o' 't. Hence I think that promise has been sometimes dear to me, ' The Lord thy God shall circumcise thy heart to love the Lord thy God.' "

The last time that I saw him on his deathbed he said to me : " Pray for me, pray for pardon, and pray for purity, for I am still in the body." A few days before his end, he said to a friend in the ministry, " I have been at the point of death, *the point of death ;*" and then raising himself, he added, " But I found that the one great mysterious death of Calvary was all I needed at the point of death." Years before, he had expressed his sense of his great unworthiness in the last of his recorded sayings in the Colloquia : " If there is anything in which I would be inclined to contradict Him, it would be if I heard Him say, ' Well done, good and faithful servant ;' " and, remarkably enough, the moment after the Lord Jesus had received his spirit, his attendant uttered over him those very words, " Well done, good and faithful servant."

The close of the forty-fifth Psalm was one of the Bible scenes on which he loved to dwell, not to open it, but to linger over it :—

> " She shall be brought unto the King in raiment of
> needlework :
> The virgins her companions that follow her shall
> be brought unto Thee.
> With gladness and rejoicing shall they be brought :
> They shall enter into the King's palace."

For the unseen and the future he liked to drink from the well of the pure Word of life, without adding words of others, or of his own, and to draw for himself thoughts sweet and many from a source that might seem to minds less thoughtful little more than " a spring shut up and a fountain sealed." These words he interpreted of the disembodied spirit carried by the angels into Abraham's bosom, and he applied them to the spirits of just men who had recently been removed from among ourselves. At the time of his own departure from this world, while remembering his application of this passage to others, and while thinking of it in connexion with himself, it seemed to me as if in the company of the blessed receiving him into the everlasting habitations, the inquiry might be made, " Who is this that cometh up from the wilderness leaning on the Beloved ?" —and that they might be answered with the reply : " This is he who when bidden to the marriage feast went and sat down in the lowest room."

CHAPTER VI.

HIS MENTAL CHARACTER.

Every man would reproduce Himself, and so change God's
beautiful diversity into a hideous uniformity.—J. D.

DR. DUNCAN had genius, a gift which requires to be shared in for its right delineation.
But, without attempting to gauge his mental
power, I may venture to offer some indications
of its character. As it seemed to me, his
leading mental characteristic was

DISCERNMENT.

In some other powers he was deficient; in
general energy, in the faculty of guiding others,
in common sense, in ability to persevere in a
prescribed path. But he far excelled most men
in intellectual discernment: in insight into
divine mystery, in understanding the truths of
theology, in penetrating the depths of philosophy, in the appreciation of poetic beauty, in
the perception of the nicest turns of speech in
every tongue, in distinguishing the character
of men taken ideally, in discrimination of
shades of sentiment, and in the faculty of
entering into manifold sympathies.

In reasoning power he may have been

equalled, or perhaps surpassed by some of his associates. His colleague in the Theological Hall, Dr. Cunningham, not only excelled him immeasurably in strength of will, energy of purpose, and general vigour of character; but although he was not so acutely, so brilliantly, and so sententiously logical, could probably have excelled him in argument, partly by innate strength of reason, and partly by greater freedom from an excessive multiplicity of ideas. Dr. Duncan's very clearness of view in reaching at once the end of a path helped to unfit him for detailing to others the steps of reasoning by which they might reach it; he had found it, but did not know what hindered you, and sometimes could not show you the intermediate process: But he far surpassed Dr. Cunningham in intellectual perception, and in the cognate capacity of fixed and intense thinking. He was master of richer and brighter mental treasures; he saw thoughts more quickly, and could surround them with light and clothe them with beauty; and he could by intuition pierce quite through into a deeper mine of thought. As regards reason, he could in no respect be compared to many of our men of physical science, in whom the faculty of observing and arranging natural facts is so admirably acute, while their faculty of reasoning on them appears so impotent. But as those accomplished men see so quickly and so deeply into the world without us, so he possessed an unrivalled insight into the inner world of thought and of higher being.

LOVE OF MYSTERY.

No man had a more intense delight in solving difficulties; he entered keenly into all the questions that have ever been raised by others, and started many more of his own; but none rested with a more child-like repose in mysteries that lay beyond solution.

To be asked questions gave him the greatest pleasure. The unwearied delight he had in searching into the roots of all things, and his faculty of answering inquiries, were such that after his death, on the suggestion of difficulties hard to be solved, the thoughts of his friends were still apt to revert naturally to him as to their counsellor, till they were recalled again to the stern reality of his absence from earth. Sometimes, indeed, he evaded an answer, as thus: "What is the meaning of the words, 'When the Comforter is come he will reprove the world of judgment'?" "I cannot answer the question, but I could make a sermon on the text." At other times he would say at once all he thought fit to express on the subject and leave it. "Is it ever lawful now to follow the example of Jonathan in asking a sign from the Lord?" "You can't lay down a law for a man when he is in straits; there is no limiting either what a man will do, or what the Lord will do for him, when refuge fails him." Most commonly, however, his reply was not the closing of your subject, but the opening of a far greater one than you had been aware of. Either he showed you that your question had been fully discussed by various authors, or else he plunged you into deeper questions which lay far below your own, and made it seem quite superficial. In either case he startled you with the amount of light he shed on what had seemed hid in thick darkness; and if you had time to wait till he returned to your starting-point, the process was as interesting as the result was instructive.

But after he had cleared the way beyond most men's line to the utmost of his own, he loved to end in mystery. Of necessity every path ends there; but he not only submitted to, but delighted in such a termination, and rested in mystery with childlike wonder and delight. It was a repose to his inmost soul, which was profoundly reverential. This combination of the inquisitive and the reverential elements, and both in the very highest degree, was one of the chief characteristics of the man.

The same power of taking in the converse of his thoughts pervaded the working of his mind in all things, whether great or little. He had been examining an ivory Indian idol with interest and inquiry; and he closed his thoughts on the curious workmanship with the remark, " But I have no doubt that it has provoked the eyes of His glory."

On the intuitional and mystical elements in his character one of his students writes from intimate knowledge : " Intuition, tending as always to mysticism, was, as I judge, the great characteristic of his mental character ; but it was checked by a high development of the logical faculty, and kept from extravagance.

The synergism of the mystical and logical tendencies produced in him the great power of resting in the delicate mean and of keeping ever the fine subjective balance. Hence his love of the 'caveats' of which he so often spoke. Hence his Hegelianism : ' There is a true as well as a false Hegelianism,' said he often, meaning by Hegelianism the balance of opposites. He liked as much of the definite as possible, because he was logical; but he loved to contemplate the infinite mystery into which it ultimately shades off, because he was intuitional and mystical. So hence, also, the Personal Jehovah was the infinite βάθος, and the Infinite βάθος the Personal Jehovah." [4]

Another intimate friend says of him, " He was at once intensely speculative and intensely devout. There was in his theologizing that union of speculative thought and devout feeling which made it attractive to two sections of Christians. The emotional prized it as a stimulus to thought. The intellectual prized it as an excitement to feeling." [12]

VARIETY.

The physical sciences in any department he could not be said to have embraced in the range of his studies; and he was very ignorant of external nature. Of mathematics one of his friends says : " In mathematics he never could progress. He specially stuck at the calculus because there lay some metaphysical flaw at the beginning which he could not supply and

which he would not pass. He refused the
system on account of the supposed defect." [10]
On his want of acquaintance with physical
science and nature another writes : " This he
regretted and had reason to regret. His mind
was too evidently turned inwards upon itself.
Mathematics, natural science, or any study that
would have made him think about the world
outside might have saved him from much
misery. Philology, philosophy, and theology,
at all events as he prosecuted them, were very
much self-contemplation and self-study. He
would have been a far happier man had he been
able, through the study of natural science, to
escape the misery of constantly thinking about
himself. He had a general feeling of the
poetry of nature, but took little interest in
particular natural objects. He was ignorant
of the names of the commonest flowers. He
used to regret that he had not attended to the
Saviour's call to ' Consider the lilies.' On the
most beautiful scenery he seldom bestowed
more than a casual glance. Once I remember
while travelling with him and his daughter on
the Greenock railway, we had a peculiarly
striking view of Dumbarton Castle. Dr.
Duncan was reading a Bohemian grammar ;
his daughter said, ' O papa, there is Dumbarton
Castle.' Without once lifting his eye from the
page, he merely said, ' I have seen Dumbarton
Castle, lassie, monie a time.' " [12]

But apart from mathematical and physical
studies, there was no sphere of intellect in
which he did not seem to be at home. A

German student said of his acquirements :
" The Germans study one thing, and know it
thoroughly ; the Scotch have a smattering of
everything, and know nothing well ; but there
is one man in Scotland, John Duncan, who
knows everything, and he knows them all
better than we know any one."

In his intellectual and moral nature his
character was many-sided. His individuality
was, indeed, strongly marked ; to find another
man like him was hopeless ; he was altogether
original and unique. " Every man would reproduce himself," was one of his acute sayings,
" and so turn God's beautiful variety into a
hideous uniformity;" there was no man whom it
would have been harder to reproduce than John
Duncan. But while his character possessed a
unity of its own, its elements were so various,
and each was so largely developed, that they
might have been thought to belong to different
men ; and if each feature were fully brought out
the character would seem fictitious, because
incompatible with itself. The simple believer,
the absorbed divine, the subtle philosopher,
the ardent and erudite linguist, the student of
a multifarious literature, the solitary recluse
and the restless lover of society, the child in
weakness of will and the man of persistent
energy, had often the aspect not merely of different but of antagonistic men. As in every
subject which he looked upon his intellect took
in elements that to simpler minds seemed contrary to each other, so his own character when
looked upon at different points seemed to pre-

sent an incongruity or a contrariety, while at the same time there was over it a conspicuous oneness.

He wanted the breadth of practical comprehensiveness ; and his mental character might have been taken for intensity and multiplicity peculiarly combined. But he possessed great width of mind ; and in every subject of inquiry he both saw it intuitively on every side, and took in the widest range of thoughts that have been brought to bear upon it by other minds.

STRENGTH OF DESIRE : WEAKNESS OF WILL.

In everyday life his will was unusually weak ; he could be easily turned from whatever he designed to do, or changed in any judgment he had formed in practical matters to be done by others. Weakness of purpose was the greatest defect in his character. Another man with a small share of his acuteness, but with more strength of will, could have got through his daily duties far more easily and more efficiently. With the same amount of desire in both for any ordinary object, the other would attain it by simple steadfastness of purpose without difficulty and without any special effort, when his vacillating will would lose it altogether.

On the other hand, in the great objects of his life he appeared to possess a singular and indomitable strength of resolution. Not one in a thousand would have pressed and persisted through the hardships of his youth in school, in college, and onwards toward the ministry, through discouragement, through poverty, through almost hopeless failure of reaching any tolerable end of his ambition. He had the same persistence in any little object for which he had a great desire; he would and did obtain it. It was the same also in his mental pursuits; in the acquisition of languages, or in reaching the utmost end of a speculative inquiry. Either there was an inward vigour of will that was only occasionally called into exercise; his will being at once both weak and strong, very weak and very strong, partly clay and partly iron: or rather, it may have been that, with a radical defect of will, his strength of desire compensated its weakness and served in its stead.

Similar in some respects was his desire to teach and his inability to rule. No pedagogue had a greater love for teaching, and no heartless and incompetent teacher had ever less faculty for governing his pupils, or indeed for guiding others in any capacity. Teaching was of the nature of a passion with him. From his student days till the end of his life he taught his pupils with ardour in his own way, however irregularly and however unsuccessfully. He taught his fellow-teachers, such as a friend in a Yorkshire school of whom he sometimes spoke, and whom he sedulously instructed in the true power of " h," till he was finally defeated by the hopeless conclusion,—" Oh, John, John, you'll never get me to haspirate the haitches." Between their engagement and their marriage he set himself most laboriously

L

to teach his first wife Greek; and at the commencement of his professorship in Edinburgh he opened a class for teaching young ladies Hebrew.   He would often teach a child, a servant, or any one whom he found willing to receive lessons in any branch of learning.   In a house where he was visiting he found that the under-kitchenmaid was ignorant of the Bible. In setting himself to teach her he kindled the anger of the cook, who locked his pupil in the scullery one day to insure her culinary diligence for a special dinner; but he ferreted out her retreat, got hold of the key, and with a large Bible in one hand and an English dictionary in the other, conducted his released prisoner to a parlour up-stairs for a quiet lesson.   But he had no power of ruling; he could keep no class in order, and was throughout his life more of the helpless child than of the teacher; yet there was a powerful element in him, which saved his intellectual activity from wasting itself in an aimless contentment with its own exercise.

In common things he was singularly dependent; in higher matters he was most deferential to authority, to Scripture absolutely, to secondary authority, as of the early Church, largely. But he was the most independent of all thinkers; he believed, or knew, that he could think all that is within the reach of human intellect, and would let no man think for him on any subject of thought.

In form his head was lofty, but decidedly small in compass.

TRANSPARENCY.

He was by far the most transparent man I have ever known. The openness of weakness in another, that wants both the desire and the power of self-concealment, and keeps nothing hidden because it has nothing to hide, was in him the transparency of a casket of precious jewels. He had intense pleasure in thinking; no other man seemed to have an equal delight in the mere exercise of the intellect: to have ceased from thought, or to have paused in thinking, would have been to him an excruciating pain. As every man influences others more by what he says to himself than by what he says to them, his visible thinking awoke thoughts in his students and his friends as no other man could; and his unconcealed moral and spiritual affections and emotions moved, as none other did, kindred emotions in the hearts of those around him. You were not, indeed, admitted to the first formation of his thoughts, or to see them unripe; and if you started a point that he had not considered, which was rare, he would probably make no reply at the moment, and answer you at another time. But when he knew his ground, he thought audibly before you; and much, both of his speech and of his preaching, was thinking aloud. Intellectually, morally, and spiritually he was the openest of men. You saw him fearing, sorrowing, believing, rejoicing; you saw him reverencing

God; you saw him under the chidings of conscience; you saw him struggling with sin; you saw him exulting in unseen glory and beauty. In his openness, as in some other features of character, he bore a true, although remote, resemblance to the great Master whom he loved; to the Son of Man who, with infinite depths of light inaccessible within him, was yet the openest and most transparent of all the sons of men.

APHORISTIC HABIT.

To this notice of his intellectual character may be added a note on one of his leading mental habits : the constant tendency of his mind to cast itself into a proverbial mould. The proverbs of others he seldom quoted, and he can scarcely be said to have fashioned new ones of his own. But the aim of the Eastern proverb, to pierce into the innate character of things, and after retracing this to its furthest issues to draw its extreme development in a short aphoristic line, was the mental exercise in which he most of all delighted. When his intellect had toiled in detecting the hidden root of whatever had appeared above - ground, he would not rest till he had cast the fruit of his search into a compact seed; into an aphorism which he could present to himself and others as embodying the substance of the matter, and out of which he could again develop it all. Six words, " Puseyism a carcase, Plymouthism a ghost," graphically describing both in their essential characters and their extreme forms, the one as wanting a soul and the other as wanting a body, give the results of long and deep thought on these two religionisms, their characteristic contrast, their inward types and inevitable developments.

" He seemed to me," writes one of his friends "to have embodied the results of his thoughts on most subjects in compendious sentences and aphorisms, which were always ready whenever he had occasion to speak on any given subject." [4] " No man," says another, " ever had a keener sense of and a greater delight in the poetry of abstract thought than he. He was, with all his stern regard to truth, an artist in his theologizing. He strove to give his thoughts a certain chaste beauty of form; some of his characteristic sayings, through being often repeated, became almost perfect in point of form." [12]

He had a fastidious sense of the music of words.

With all his love of speech, he was able to exercise a rare silence. His interview with the Archduke of Hungary (p. 66) never came to be known in the mission, and was only surmised in the family from his dress on the occasion : " He was markedly silent about it, and unexpectedly wise. He could be silent in as many languages as he could speak." [10]

CHAPTER VII.

LEADING MORAL FEATURES.

Christ came to save the contrasts of Himself; but not to leave
them such. There's nobody perfect: That's the believer's
bed of thorns: That's the hypocrite's couch of ease.—J. D.

"CHRIST is a study" was the great opening
sentence of one of his sermons ; and there was
nothing in him more remarkable than

HIS LOVE TO JESUS CHRIST.

Jesus Christ, in his person, his character, his
life, his death, was the central subject of his
thoughts, and increasingly year by year till
the end. It was not theology but Christ
that filled both his mind and his heart; the
whole stream of his theology sprang from Him
as its source and flowed to him as its ocean.
The holy Lord God of his earlier years was his
fear and his delight to the last, and it was ever
true of him that " he feared God above many ;"
but in the latter portion of his life, Jesus Christ
was peculiarly the one object of his desires and
the constant subject of his meditation.

"What would we do without Christ?" he
said to me a year before his death. "About

the miracles I am not a right believer. I
believe the miracles; but I believe in the
miracles on account of Christ, instead of believing in Christ on account of the miracles.
Christ is a wonderful Being; we could never
do without Christ." I replied, " Your believing is of the very best kind, for Christ himself
says, ' Believe me, that I am in the Father and
the Father in me, *or else* believe me for the
very works' sake.' "

Again he said, " We make far too little of
the Incarnation; the Fathers knew much more
of the incarnate God. Some of them were
oftener at Bethlehem than at Calvary; they
had too little of Calvary, but they knew Bethlehem well. They took up the Holy Babe in
their arms; they loved Immanuel, God with
us. We are not too often at the cross, but we
are too seldom at the cradle; and we know
too little of the Word made flesh, of the Holy
Child Jesus."

It was the same absorbing devotion to Jesus
Christ that made the angel whom he loved
best, and most longed to see out of all the
heavenly host, to be the one who was honoured
with the ministration of " strengthening his
Lord in the garden;" that Lord himself so
supremely beloved, and most of all in his dying
love, that for his sake he loved the messenger
who ministered to him in the hour of his
weakness and sorrow.

This interest in Christ rose above every
passing interest of earth. In the questions of
the day he took a lively concern; not in party

politics, on which I never heard him utter a word in the midst of all his talk, but in all subjects of national welfare. A friend met him on the street at a time of some public interest, and not in mere form asked him, " Is there any news to-day ?" " O yes," he replied, " this is always news, The blood of Jesus Christ cleanseth us from all sin."

HIS LOVE TOWARD ALL MEN.

He embodied in a singularly fine example the beautiful contrast brought out in the apostolic words, " In understanding be men, but in malice be ye children." No truer or more characteristic description could have been written of John Duncan than this : " In understanding a man, in malice a child ;" and the moral feature was quite as marked as the intellectual. It would be hard to find a man who had through grace more completely " put off anger, wrath, malice, and all bitterness." It was not that he looked on sin simply in the abstract, shunning to condemn the sinner together with the sin. He would quote such a sentence as this, " If thou take forth the wicked from the righteous, there shall come forth a vessel for the finer," and would say, " Such texts mean not the destruction of wickedness, but of wicked men : 'God putteth away all the wicked of the earth as dross.'" Nor had he any part in that easy good-nature which is little disturbed by evil anywhere, within or without ; for he had a severe and life-long struggle with sin. But unlike the good men, who while severe to themselves are also stern towards others, he was full of tenderness and love ; grace in him presented a man singularly free from bitterness and ill-will and every element of strife and contention. " Hateful haters !" he said, " a world of hateful haters ! Is not this world thus a forehall, an antechamber of hell ?"

As pertaining to strife, he had a great aversion to lawsuits in every form and for any object; and he appeared to hold them to be unlawful in Christians. Of what he called " the horrors of war," he spoke with a shuddering sensitiveness, as if he felt the sword piercing his own soul at the moment. He sometimes praised the success of the passive principles of the Quakers; and when he had occasion to commend those who took up arms in defence of the true religion, he was careful to add that he highly honoured them notwithstanding this earthly warfare, and not on account of it; yet he neither justified nor expressly condemned that part of their course. But when under Napoleon III. the invasion of England had at one time become a subject of alarm and of conversation, he was not only cordial in approving of all military preparations, but was amusingly ardent, for a man of his habits, in his profession of readiness to become a soldier : " I would go out into the field myself," he said with much animation, " and fight for my country."

His love toward all men, and his want of all

malice, were specially brought out in his singular freedom from the vice of evil-speaking.
This was the more noteworthy because "much
speaking" was a frequent snare to him. In
speaking at inconvenient times and at excessive length, he forgot the counsel of a wiser
than himself, that "in the multitude of words
there wanteth not sin;" although in speaking
to God he often remembered the higher warning, "God is in heaven, and thou on earth,
therefore let thy words be few." But as regards "backbiting with the tongue, and taking
up a reproach against a neighbour," the com-
mendation might fitly be bestowed on him,
"If any man offend not in word, the same is a
perfect man." This perfect "bridling of the
tongue" from speaking evil was the more
trying in his case, and its mastery a greater
triumph, because he did not limit himself to
the rule of saying nothing about your neighbour except when you can speak well of him.
Toward his neighbour he bridled his tongue
with a perfect control and skill, but he did not
muzzle it. Talking about his fellow-men was
in mere bulk a very small ingredient of his
multitudinous speech. But he delighted in
portraying men's characters; not in gossip,
not in long discussion, and not in random
remarks, but in one or two deep lines of a
portrait thoughtfully fashioned in his own
mind, as he abridged a subject into its most
practical shape, so he condensed a man into an
aphoristic sentence. He greatly loved to
dwell on the good that was in men, but it was

the characteristic good; and he shunned the
utterance of any evil, so far as it was mixed
with the "leaven of malice." Yet he characterized the man, not as good, and not as bad,
but as an individual human being with his
own distinctiveness; painting the portrait in
vivid hues, but never mingling his colours with
any drops of "the poison that is under the
tongue."

"The command," he said, is not 'Thou shalt
love thyself as thy neighbour;' but, 'Thy
neighbour as thyself.' There is a priority, but
a priority among equals.—The Talmud says :
He who says, 'Mine is mine and thine is thine,'
is a just man ; he who says, 'Mine is mine and
thine is mine,' is a wicked man; but he who
says, 'Thine is thine and mine is thine,' is a
good man.—Love seeketh not her own. Some
people's minds are made up of extreme suspi-
ciousness. If they hear part of a matter concerning any one, and there be both a clean
and a dirty handle to take hold of it by, they
are sure to take hold of it by the dirty handle.
If you are without love, then the church bell is
as good a Christian as you."

HIS LOVE OF HOLINESS.

The unalterable and absolutely beautiful Law
of God was his great root-principle ; it was the
object of his enthusiastic and boundless admiration. Antinomianism was the object of his
dread, loathing, and hatred ; he marked its
subtle approaches with a wakeful jealousy ; and

he met it with an intense enmity when he discovered it seducing himself, or stealing upon
his friends unsuspected by themselves or by
others.   He was jealous of part of the present
lay preaching, as tinged with a less common
form of error, which he characterized as an
" Arminian antinomianism."   So also he was
afraid of mere comfort.   " Unmixed joy, that
is not for earth ; that hath never been on the
earth since Adam fell, unless, perhaps, in the
Man of Sorrows, after His resurrection, when
the load was off.   Purifying work is sorrowful
work : sorrow at the thought of being impure,
yet joy at the thought of coming purity." [15]

His love of holiness was brought out further
in his strong views of Conscience.   " If you
address children," he said, " you will find that
what lays hold on them is everything that
appeals to the conscience."   In speaking of
men whose views of redemption were not very
clear, but who were deeply conscientious, he
said, " I can scarcely think that a man will
perish who has a tender conscience."

He was humbler than other men, because
his perception of holiness was clearer and his
love of holiness more intense, and because there
was no child of God on earth whom he looked
on as so far from having attained it as himself.
He used to say, " It 's best not to fall, but if
you fall be sure to rise again ; ' A just man
falleth seven times and riseth again ;' ' These
things write we unto you that *ye sin not ;* and
if any man sin, we have an Advocate with the
Father.' "

No man oftener described, or seemed to know so thoroughly, the conflict between the old man and the new in the child of God. A Bible, that excluded the child of God from the seventh chapter of the Epistle to the Romans, would have been a strange and dark book to him. He would exclaim with a jubilant voice, " I delight in the law of God after the inward man ;" and would add, " But some men have no inner man," that being peculiar to the believer in Christ. But again the cry, " O wretched man that I am ! who shall deliver me from the body of this death ?" was wrung out from the depths of a heart in which there was a perpetual war between good and evil. He read the words, " When Christ, who is our life, shall appear, then shall ye also appear with him in glory. Mortify therefore your members which are upon the earth ; fornication, uncleanness, inordinate affection, evil concupiscence, and covetousness, which is idolatry," and he exclaimed, " What a Head ! and what members !"

In answer to the question, " Can the tempting of Satan be distinguished from the seduction of sin ?" he started up and replied, " O yes ; I've caught him at it, I've caught him at it." But his strength lay in bringing out Paul's personification of Sin. In his preaching you witnessed the noble and inspiriting sight, not of a picture of the field of battle, but rather of a portion of the great battle-field between evil and good, between gigantic evil and omnipotent good. The hearer was led into the heart of the conflict, and found himself standing in the great death-battle; in the scene of the last struggle of evil for existence, with all its terrible strength put forth before surrendering its life, and of the believer's triumphant victory through his Lord Jesus Christ. "Will the σάρξ (the carnal mind)," he asked, "lie down and submit to be slaughtered like a lamb? No, it will resist to the very last; it will only yield when grace has conquered it." It was one of the peculiar and almost inimitable excellences of his preaching, that while he did not refer to his own past experience in the way of narrative, he enacted it over again at the moment, and intertwined it with the thread of a discourse that appeared to contain no personal reference.

But while he knew well that the war between good and evil in the child of God would never cease on earth, he was so jealous of holiness, and so earnest for its cultivation, that he did not care to speak strongly against the doctrine of Christian perfectibility in this world. "I have less quarrel," he said, "with a man holding the doctrine of perfection; but I would not like to see the man who thinks himself perfect." He wished all men to press as near to perfection as they could; and with his marked dislike to Wesleyan views on most points, and specially disagreeing with them regarding the old and new man in the believer, he would quote with zest their reproach against Calvinism, that "Death is the Genevan purgatory." The substance of his own creed was,

" There 's nobody perfect ; that 's the believer's bed of thorns ; that 's the hypocrite's couch of ease." Among his last words on his deathbed he said, " Pray for me, pray for pardon, pray for purity."

HIS HUMILITY.

The most marked of all the moral features in Dr. Duncan's character was humility. He was singularly humble, in consideration of his great talents, of his vast treasures of learning, and of his attainments in the divine life. But if we set all these aside, and compare him with other Christian men, we cannot but come to the conclusion that out of all the guests bidden in these days by the King within the circle of our knowledge, it was he that took the lowest room at the feast. It was not that he was unconscious of his talents, or disposed to undervalue his attainments. He knew that he could justify his excessive share of all conversation only on the ground of his thoughts being of more value than most other people's ; and he rather liked to refer to his candidature for the Oriental Chair in the University of Glasgow, when he made an offer for examination in Hebrew Literature in which he knew that no man there was competent to test him. He would quote with a simple pride a sentence in his letter of application, in which in the event of failure he comforted himself with the thought that " Sparta had found a better man ;" but with the evident consciousness that for such a position

there was no better man to be found in Sparta.
But with all his consciousness of intellectual
power and literary attainment, the "clothing
of humility" covered him from head to foot as
it did no other man.

This lowliness was allied to the childlike
simplicity which pervaded his whole Christian
course, and was made more evident by the
helplessness which rendered him so unfit to
guide himself in common matters, and so willing to be guided by others. But its root lay
in his sense of the majesty of God, which was
far more profound than in other men, and
humbled him lower in the dust ; in his perception and his love of holiness, and the consciousness of his own defect ; in his sense of
ingratitude for the unparallelled love of the
Lord Jesus Christ, and in his abiding conviction of past sin and of present sinfulness. This
habitual humbling was deepened by the wounding of his very tender conscience, through yield-
ing himself to be carried away by what chanced
to take hold of his mind.

These combined elements rendered him an
example of an altogether rare and inimitable
humility. Men who may be reckoned holier
might be named out of those who served the
Lord along with him ; but among them all it
would be hard to find one so humble. The
holiness of Robert M'Cheyne, if not so deep,
was more equal, and more thoroughly leavened
the character hour by hour. The holiness of
William Burns was in some respects as deep,
and it was singularly constant. They were both

more watchful, and therefore more evenly holy. But in the race to stoop down into their Lord's sepulchre, John Duncan outran them both; he was the humblest of the three, and of all the men whom most of us have known.

His sitting down among the inquirers at Kilsyth in 1839, and his resuming a similar posture elsewhere at an interval of nearly thirty years, are not to be ascribed to mere anxiety and doubt about his own salvation. Of such doubt he had often more than enough. But the act was also one of simple, childlike, genuine humility, and the fruit of deep self-abasement. When seated at the Lord's Table with his own intense desire, if there had been a place at once inside and outside of the guests, David's welcomed place as " a doorkeeper in the house of God," that of all others would have been his chosen seat, the fittest and the happiest place for him as the " chief of sinners," as " less than the least of all saints."

M

CHAPTER VIII.

THEOLOGICAL VIEWS.

The people of God are a plain people; and doctors of divinity,
when they go out of this plainness, must be shoved to a lower
form.—J. D.

"HE revelled in the metaphysics of theology," writes one of his intimate friends. "He
was a philosophical sceptic, but he never ceased
to philosophize. He renounced philosophy as
an authority, but never ceased to regard her
as a helper in the study of divine truth. He
thirsted for the absolute certainty which no
philosophy gives. He put questions which to
every philosophy lie unanswered. Such as—
'How can the trustworthiness of my senses be
established? How can the objective validity of
thought or a system of thought be proved beyond
question?' His view coincided with that of
Röthe, that the trustworthiness of our senses and
the objective validity of consciousness must be
problematic except on theological grounds. In
regard to every conclusion of philosophy he
said '_dubito_.' His thirst for absolute certainty was satisfied only by divine authority—

178

in Scripture. And yet he used to say, ' Baptize philosophy; let her be called Mary, *ancilla Domini*. She may serve but must not rule in Christ's house.' " [12]

" You are an untrained theologue," he said in my house to Mr. Brownlow North. " Very untrained," was his reply. " You mistake me, sir; I laid the emphasis not on ' untrained ' but on ' theologue.' " He spoke of Mr. North as a " born theologian," and often said to me very earnestly, " You should advise Brownlow North. to study theology." Of some other preachers he would say, " He 'll never make a theologian; he should not try it; there is no theology in him."

He was himself both a theologian born, and a theologian trained, with few equals either in the natural faculty for the science, or in its cultivation by manifold learning. Men great in theology are often supposed to possess minds naturally dry and hard, however acute; but Dr. Duncan presented a magnificent example of the brightest genius combined with the highest theological talent. His delight in every theological thought from the weightiest doctrine down to the mint and the anise and the cummin, his love for the words of ancient creeds, his long citations from ecclesiastical councils stored in a marvellous memory, his profound knowledge of systems of theology and his exhaustless reading in its authors, his subtle theological definitions, and his bright theological oracles, marked him as distinctively and eminently a theologian. A few words from this "master of sentences" have conveyed to many minds a new conception of the study; they had seen and heard a theologian,—a character of man which they had seldom met before, and never in so normal a type.

THE SCRIPTURES.

"The Word of God is in your mouth" he often told as Malan's pointed address to him on the day of his conversion, and with it his own prayer: "And may he not take it utterly out of my mouth." His after experience was a continuous fulfilment of the promise to his Redeemer: "My words which I have put in thy mouth shall not depart out of thy mouth, nor out of the mouth of thy seed."

"The words of the Holy Ghost" was the designation by which he delighted to call the books of the Old and New Testament Scriptures. Very few men, indeed, have possessed equal talents for entering into the different characters of the various writers of Scripture, or for criticising their respective styles; and he spoke quite freely of "the genius of Paul," and of "the long stretches of Isaiah." But he presented a fine contrast to the flippancy of many modern theologians, who seat themselves in the throne of God, and constitute themselves judges of what in his Book is right and what is wrong, according to their own capricious and perverted tastes. His creed and his words were, "All Scripture is given by inspiration of God," and "Every word of God is

pure." He said to his students—" The Spirit
of God makes known the things of God, as
things given of God to those to whom the
Spirit is given to know these. We must
observe this enclosing language of Holy Scripture ; we must not look beyond, but in the
Scripture, and we will find that every passage
either proves itself or is proved by parallelism.
Hereby we know that we know him, by his
Spirit that he hath given to us ; the things
revealed by the Spirit the Apostles spake.
God employs human speech ; but he himself
selects the words that are to express his
thoughts. He leaves not man to put words
on them ; the words are as much the Spirit's
as the ideas, and the Apostle Paul studiously
avoids other words." [1]

" Some one passage of Scripture, often the
essence of some hundred unconnected texts, is
given as a remedy to the diseased soul." [15]

But while many agree with him in an un-
feigned and a candid acceptance of the Holy
Scriptures as inspired throughout, he was the
only man I ever knew who appeared to me to
believe and to love every word of God without
preferring one above another. In interpreting
a text he excelled even Calvin in his freedom
from bias in favour of other texts. He held
Christ's death for the elect, and delighted in it
as the corner-stone of the great temple. But
such a verse as " God so loved the world, that
he gave his only begotten Son, that whosoever
believeth in him should not perish, but have
everlasting life," he could not bear to be inter-

preted of the " elect world ;" an interpretation
of which he said, " It makes nonsense of the
text." In like manner was his reply to the
question, " Is the common interpretation of
1 John i. 9 just in limiting to the children of
God exclusively the words, ' If we confess our
sins, he is faithful and just to forgive us our
sins, and to cleanse us from all unrighteous-
ness,' when the verse preceding is, ' If we say
that we have no sin, we deceive ourselves, and
the truth is not in us,' and the verse following,
' If we say that we have not sinned, we make
him a liar, and the truth is not in us' ?" He
answered, " No ; that text must take in men
in general : *we* in these verses is just the
French *on.*"

So with every text, with doctrine, with
promise, with precept, he received and loved
each one as if it had been his special choice,
taking in the most widely different thoughts
in a manner to most minds impossible. " The
Scripture cannot be broken" was his great
dogma ; and his childlike reception of different
texts, without mutilating any of them, helped
him toward discovering the fulness of their
beautiful harmony in the mind of their Divine
author.

On the subject of Inspiration I asked him,
" When the Prophets narrate events as in their
own persons, which appear to pertain only to
the Lord Jesus Christ, as David in the 22d
Psalm, what do you suppose was their own
state of mind, or their relation to what they
uttered ?" He answered, " I believe they

were brought into a state of sympathy with the experiences which they describe."

Without knowing him in his earlier years, I came to the conclusion that he must always have possessed an unusual amount of candour, for he might be said to be even too candid in argument. He admired and delighted in a good reason against himself; and he would yield to a wrong one which he could not answer at the moment, when a man of duller mind would have distrusted his own acuteness, and have still believed in the goodness of his cause although he could not prove it. " I would have been a Socinian, but could not for the Greek article, and so I became a Sabellian," exhibited the natural candour of his mind as a student; and the same disposition sanctified by grace pervaded his interpretation of Scripture throughout his life.

The clearness of his intellect seemed to carry him into a region where various difficulties, which looked irreconcileable to others, had no existence. But his great strength lay in his childlike submission to God speaking in his word. To him the Bible was alone and altogether The Book. The expositions of theologians he was far indeed from undervaluing ; and to a friend, who in argument on some Scriptural truth would lay it down as a condition that the opinions of commentators should be excluded, he replied, " That is to assume that you have a monopoly of the Word of God." But you might hear him complain, " I hurt my conscience yesterday by reading an erroneous book, and I have not got myself right again." In commending a Latin theological book to me, he opened it and held it out in his hands with the remark, "You may judge that it is good, by the number of texts that are quoted." Poole's Latin Synopsis, with its unfailing store of the best that has been written on each text before or since, was the commentary which he oftenest recommended ; and he would sometimes make a student promise to him to purchase it. But of the Divine Word itself he could most sincerely say, " Oh how I love thy law, it is my meditation all the day : how sweet are thy words unto my taste, yea, sweeter than honey to my mouth : thy testimonies have I taken as an heritage for ever, for they are the rejoicing of my heart."

More than any man I ever knew, he trusted every word, reverenced every word, and loved every word in the Book of God.

While the Hebrew and Greek Scriptures were continually in his mind, he admired and loved our English Bible. "Oh, it is a pitiable thing," he exclaimed, "for a poor silly puppy of a sciolist to stand up in the pulpit vexing the people by shaking their confidence in our good English translation." [15] On its language he said to me, "I have often tried to find the rhythm of our English Bible, and have never been able to make it out; but there is a rhythm running through it."

The following remarks on the Bible are collected from notes of his addresses, taken evidently with much fidelity, by one of his students :—" Before me is a book. What is a book ? A book represents written and spoken language, which represents thought, which represents objects.—The evidence for Scripture is Scripture ; as for other evidences, what is a farthing candle in the light of the sun ? but the light of Scripture is only shown by the light that is in Christ. The true Scripture is in the saving faith of our common people ; they don't believe without evidence, but believe the truth by its own evidence. The external evidences had an influence on my mind, however, before the internal.—Consider the Bible as the word of the Living GOD ; what a majesty is in God ! 'I will hear what God the Lord will speak.'—A father's letter can be understood by the family better than outside ; but there may be things which the family don't precisely understand. The people of God are a plain people, and doctors of divinity, when they go out of this plainness, must be shoved to a lower form.

" The Bible is not a congeries of books, but a unit, with organic and vital unity ; not a lump, but an organism inspired by the Spirit of truth and Spirit of life : 'lively oracles.' The Old Testament is an imperfect unit ; in the New Testament all is either explanation or augmentive development. The Old Testament together with the New Testament is an organic whole ; they correspond as lock and key ; as building and scaffolding ; the egg and the chicken (in regard to the vitalism in Judaism). To understand the whole we must understand the parts, and conversely; just as we can't understand anatomy without physiology. —Jesus Christ, being the corner-stone, unites the prophets to the apostles. — Scripture always implies a man of God. We have no *spiritual* words in common speech; the dust of the earth is an integral part of us; the dust of the earth is on the throne of the Majesty on High.—The *modus* (manner) of plenary inspiration is incomprehensible, and not only so, but the *modus* of all Divine action is incomprehensible. All action of the Infinite on the finite must be apprehensible but not comprehensible. Moses testified of Christ; but we can rise above means, and believe Christ for himself. The sun is about to rise; there are specks of light. The sun rises, and we see him.

"'Search the Scriptures,' they testify of me; and ye, though in them ye think ye have eternal life, will not come unto me. Eternal life is in Christ, and the Scriptures contain this, and therefore Him, and this of course figuratively, using the means for the end. Eternal life is in Christ, and is He. This is a matter of Christ's honour or dishonour: of our life or death. Christ is glorious: life is sweet.

"The Bible is the best *school-book;* not only for teaching things belonging to the inner and future, but also for the outer and present life. There is no school-book in the world containing so many roots of things in so short a compass. Add to your faith universal γνῶσις (knowledge)." [5]

THE PERSON OF CHRIST.

He believed Christ to be truly God and
truly man, and yet one Christ, with an apprehension rarely equalled or approached; and
this habit, not of walking in the middle at
equal distance from two truths and finding
neither, but of embracing and combining both,
he carried with him through all theology. The
subject of the Person of Christ always occupied
a large portion of his thoughts. The oneness
of his Person in his two natures, in which many
see only a true statement into which there can
be little further inquiry, was to him a subject
of intense and constant study; and he often
opened it from such words as these,—"Who
his own self bare our sins in his own body on
the tree;" not the mere body bearing them,
but Himself bearing them in his own body;
not the human nature suffering by itself, but
He suffering in his human nature. "Crucified
in weakness" was a testimony much in his
heart and often on his lips. He loved to ponder
it, and in trying to think it out for himself
he asked a brother in the ministry, "What
is the meaning of the text, 'crucified in
weakness'?" His friend said, "It refers to
Christ's human nature." "Yes," he replied,
"but we must not evacuate the meaning of a
text." "Christ crucified," he said again, "is
the centre of Christology."

He often lamented the defective knowledge
of some of our ministers on the Person of

Christ. He said that while they would be far from defending any error, but would be zealous for the truth, they had not studied the doctrine so as to understand it; and that in distinguishing the human nature from the Divine, they so expressed themselves as to divide Christ in two : " They mean to be sound, but they are Nestorians without knowing it." He complained that when he corrected them he found his labour hopeless ; for when they had thankfully accepted his suggestion, and had seen the mistake, they altered it only by substituting another. It must be owned that, both in this and other theological truths, it was not easy for our ablest ministers to preserve a diction to which he would find no exception. But there was no man whom it was more pleasant for any of his brethren in the ministry to have as a hearer. He was the most devout and childlike listener in the whole church, and the most anxious to profit by the sermon. In going into church he would say with great delight, " Now, we 'll have some sweet Christian experience from John Milne ; he keeps his theology right by his experience."

" In Psalm ii. we have Christ as the Messiah, the Son of God, the inheritor of all nations : in Psalm viii. we have Christ as man, the Son of Man, made Lord of all : in Psalm cx. we have Christ as David's Lord, at God's right hand, till all things are under his feet —' Thou art my Son.' Is the Sonship of Christ decretive ? It is a begotten Sonship ; not at the Incarnation, for then God became man, man did not become God; not at the Resurrection, for then he was declared, not constituted Son of God with power. It is not one act or work, but eternal, timeless. 'As the Father hath life in himself, so hath he given to the Son to have life in himself,' I consider, along with the Fathers, as referring to the eternal generation of Christ. 'Life in himself' is the characteristic of God; it is a continual begetting, so that he ever says, 'This day have I begotten thee.' A figurative Son is not a begotten Son, and figurative generation is not begetting a son." [13]

On the Divinity of Christ, in answer to the Arian objection founded on 1 Tim. i. 17, where the Father is called "the only (wise) God," he cited Rev. i. 11, where Jesus calls himself "the First," quoting these words from some divine: "Primus sed non ante Patrem; solus sed non sine Filio (the First, yet not before the Father; alone yet not without the Son)."

" I am inclined to think that the great end of human redemption is the full manifestation, as of the Divine perfections, so of the Divine Tri-unity."

THE OUTPOURING OF THE SPIRIT.

" We are not thirsty yet," he said in speaking of prayer for the Holy Spirit. " How do you know?" " Because it is written, 'I will pour water upon him that is thirsty,' and 'When the poor and needy seek water, and there is none, and their tongue faileth for thirst, I the Lord will hear them, I the God of Jacob will not forsake them :' if our tongue were failing for thirst, we should have the water.—We live under the Pentecostal economy of the Holy Ghost; what was done that day was but the opening scene. It was a splendid opening no doubt, but it was the splendid entering in of a perpetuity. The Spirit takes this poor feeble humanity of ours; and when we cannot utter a prayer, He strikes out in a groan.—You intend to believe in Christ; but if you grieve the Spirit, and he takes his final departure, where will you get your faith? seeing that Christ's Bride gets hers in the effectual calling of the Holy Ghost. Oh, tempt Him not; Christ hath dignity, and he is aware of his dignity."

CALVINISM.

Divine sovereignty held a first and a large place both in his creed and in his thoughts; in his spiritual distress he found rest only by absolute submission to God as "having mercy on whom he will have mercy." He was a high Calvinist, or to speak with greater precision, a strong Calvinist; with a Calvinism cordially believed, firmly held, and consistently carried out. But although more strongly Calvinistic than most of his brethren in Scotland, he often spoke against the ultra-Calvinism which is to be found in England, while he highly esteemed some of those who held it. What he specially disliked was its tendency to Antinomianism, its withholding the free offer of the gospel, and its not laying upon all men the responsibility of repentance and of the use of the means of grace. One of his students writes that he often said, " The vanishing point of all mysteries is the ' voluntas creata.' What is a voluntas creata? (a created will). He was wont to compare the majesty of the ' fatis avolsa voluntas' (the will free from fate) on the one hand, and the divine prescience on the other, to an arch of which the keystone was unseen." [4]

Contrasting a monotonous Gospel with extreme Calvinism, he said, " Mere Evangelism sets before men an open door, but when you have gone through it you find nothing ; there is no house to the door. Ultra-Calvinism is a beautiful palace without a door ; the house is perfect, but there is no getting into it.—One kind of Antinomianism says nothing but Come ; another kind refuses to say Come ; the last is the worst of the two, because it lays no responsibility on the sinner.—The English ultra-Calvinists receive all the answers to the questions in our Shorter Catechism except one : ' To escape the wrath and curse of God due to us for sin, God requireth of us faith in Jesus Christ, repentance unto life, with the diligent use of all the outward means whereby Christ communicateth to us the benefits of redemption.' "

In reference to the free invitation of the gospel, he was fond of saying : " Christ casts out none that come to him ; but he searches all that come."

Grace was to him sovereign, supreme, and alone : "Let the natural man do his utmost," he said strongly, "he is just a well-washed sow." "Yet," he said again, "nature commonly reaches its highest at the point where grace meets it;" and he had a high respect, amounting to reverence, for the king-like liberty of the human will as above being forced. In another aspect of the will he said, "What a power there is in the will!" Being in bed with serious illness, he had been vexed with his imagination breaking loose, and with the unsanctified thoughts of his dreams. This humbled him by showing the evil that was still in his heart; but he said, "It is the imagination free from the control of the will; it is not willing sin; when we are awake the will controls the thoughts, but in sleep the will loses its dominion. We owe much to the power of the will."

His aversion to Arminianism was intense, it might be said extreme; this dislike, though modified, was not removed by its taking the most evangelical type; and he said to me earnestly a few months before his death, "Never admit an Arminian into your pulpit." But he had a warm love to all Christians notwithstanding doctrinal differences. "A word that seemed to slight any of the prerogatives or perfections of God excited his keenest feeling. He was jealous as an Old Testament prophet for Jehovah. He saw in Arminianism a systematic and plausible attack upon the divine sovereignty; and as often as

it came up he assailed it with remorseless
logic. He was a keen, but not a violent con-
troversialist. The captain of a vessel in which
he was sailing from Leith to Hamburg, he said,
once rebuked his overkeenness in controversy.
The captain was a Wesleyan; and Dr. Duncan
assailed his Arminianism without mercy. The
seaman of course was no match for the theologian, and said at last, 'I have really enough
to do, Sir, to fight with the world, the flesh,
and the devil, and I shall not fight any longer
with you.' His own views were clear, con-
sistent, and sharply defined. Yet he made
generous allowance for indefiniteness and inconsistency of view in others. He acknowledged the one faith, amid the evident diver-
gencies, and even when held along with
dangerous error. He said of a Protestant
maid-servant who was converted by the Bava-
rian priest Martin Boos, 'I do not regret her
conversion to Popery, for I believe it was her
conversion to Christ.' He said that to true
Christians who had fallen into grievous error
the Saviour's promise might apply, Mark xvi.
18, 'If they drink any deadly thing, it shall
not hurt them.'" [12]

In stating the more awful doctrines of Scripture he was very tender, and his rule regarding
them was, "In preaching these doctrines never
go beyond what can be proved by the express
words of the Bible."

Any simple statement of the Gospel had a
great attraction for him, and the simpler it was
he enjoyed it the more, if it was not contro-

versial but the genuine utterance of the heart. The account of redemption from the lips of an African woman, a slave, impressed him deeply; he liked to repeat it in conversation, and on one occasion at a meeting for prayer, he stood up and said without further remark of his own : " I have never heard the gospel better stated than it was put by a poor negress : ' Me die, or He die ; He die, me no die.'"

PRAYER.

" Fervent prayer moves the hand which moves not the heavens only, but the heart of man."

The following incidents and remarks belong rather to previous portions of these memorials, but are introduced here because received too late for insertion in their own place :—

" In a walk following a casual meeting on the street, I put the question, whether such an invitation as that, ' Ask and ye shall receive,' was for disciples or for all; and, after some conversation, more pointedly—' Might one, not knowing or thinking himself as yet a disciple or believer, take up that invitation and promise and plead it in prayer ?' After a moment of pause he said—' Yes ; but only at the footstool of a sovereign God.'" [15]

" At the time when we resided together in the same house at Pesth, Dr. Duncan, one day when conducting family worship, prayed at very great length. Apprehensive that he had encroached on other duties, he thought that some sort of apology was necessary. With the look of a child who has committed a fault, or rather with the same look which I have often seen him exhibit when he had needlessly lingered over some work to the inconvenience of others, after rising from his knees, he said, 'I fear I have been very long to-day, but when one thinks he has got in, it is very difficult to get out again.'

"His prayers were frequently lengthy from an opposite cause, because he failed to find access. The great length of his sermons was usually due to both causes combined ;—the first part being prolonged, to use his own expression, by the difficulty of getting in, and the second by the equal difficulty of getting out." [19]

"Pray for me," he said in an address to his students in 1857, "I wish to throw myself on your prayers. Not in that general way in which everybody says, 'Oh yes, we have all need of one another's prayers,' but I wish you to pray for me *that my faith fail not.* Not that I have any *positive* doubt, but my faith is very feeble ; make that the subject of your prayers.

"I am not *certain* of irregeneracy, nor do I doubt the sufficiency of the mercy of God, for it is a Perfection in Him, and all these are Infinite, neither do I doubt the regenerating power of the Spirit, but I doubt of my own regeneracy.

"There is but one condition of salvation— 'If I will :' 'I will have mercy on whom I will have mercy.' That text is full of awe, but it is one of my grounds of hope, for God there says that he will exercise his mercy and grace. We dare not say that God's mercy is not above our sin, which, though infinite, is yet finite in some respects; but God's mercy is infinite, therefore our finite sin cannot be urged against his infinite mercy, and none of us dare say that our sins exceed the righteousness of Christ. Nothing that I have done or am, if THOU pleasest, can prevent Thee from showing me mercy. And yet I am not certain of irregeneracy. I have a lingering hope still, but not a *certainty* of the salvation of my soul. What are the causes of that non-compliance with God's call—'My son, give me thine heart?' —a divided heart, whorish and unstable in keeping God's covenant. 'When He slew them then they inquired after them, but they soon forgot His mighty works.' And, gentlemen, let me tell you to beware of that in which I have failed and offended; beware of resting short of giving the whole heart unto God. Conversion is a great work of God, and of man under the mighty power of the Holy Ghost; a divine work upon a rational being having an understanding, will, and affections. Hence 'Turn ye, turn ye,' and also the souls' cry, 'Turn us and we shall be turned.' Yea, that very command, 'Make you a new heart' must be obeyed. 'Ye have purified your hearts, keep yourselves in the love of God,' all these things must be done. Make not slim work of conversion. Give *the whole heart as it is;* we must give God the *wicked* heart. It is then unbelief comes in. One thing I must tell you: Abuse not reliefs; grieve not the Holy Ghost. It's that I have done. Linguistic studies have occupied more of my life and more of my heart than they should have done.

" In giving yourselves wholly to the Lord your walk will be comfortable and happy, a way of pleasantness. But how deceitful is the heart and desperately wicked! Our lusts come upon us, and they may be lawful things on which they are set, things not in themselves sinful, obtaining the praise of men, even of good men. They are lawful, and you like them, but it is not God's will that you should do them. You won't give up your god nor your self-will. You won't consent to give the whole heart, nor quit His service altogether; you begin to serve two masters, convictions are stifled, prayer is restrained, and an evil conscience tells you that you are mocking God, that your God is a necessity, that He has become to you a necessary evil. What are you doing then? You are reversing your religion, mocking your God instead of adoring him and serving him. If we be His, it comes to this, that he will endure no longer, and he brings us that we can endure no longer. Being intolerable to Him, he makes our way intolerable to ourselves. Oh! I can't endure to hate God any longer. It's shameful treatment of the Holy One. I'm seeing sin as sin, wherefore I abhor myself and repent.

" My soul expects to hear only the voice of pardon as it says 'I will return,' but the Lord meets it with the voice of rebuke and reproof : ' I will reprove thee, and set thy ways in order

before thine eyes—consider this, ye that forget
God, lest I tear in pieces, and there be none
to deliver.' I have often been brought to consider this text so far as a promise. He doesn't
say absolutely, I will tear in pieces, but Consider this lest I do it. It's *great* forgiveness
He bestows, and he'll have us know this by
setting the greatness of our sins before us.

" And now my position is this : He is order-
ing my ways before me, and I ask your prayers
that my faith fail not. God's gracious dealings
with me in the past are aggravations of my sin.
Don't make use of past evidences of grace
against present charges of sin. To the Mercy
of God and the Blood of Sprinkling! Evidences are good in their own place, but shall a
man palliate his guilt by pleading how gracious
God has been to him?" [20]

CHAPTER IX.

VIEWS ON THE CHURCH.

Puseyism a carcase : Plymouthism a ghost.—J. D.

"THE Bishops themselves," he said, "are always Presbyterians on an ordination day. But I think we give a less place to the Congregation than it has in the New Testament;" meaning by congregation not the people specially, but the individual Church, consisting of ministers, elders, and members. Referring to the reformation of the ancient Armenian Church in Turkey, he wrote: "Was not the primitive Church-government parochial episcopacy? and should not, if possible, and if no evil is likely to arise, the term bishop be retained? Its extension to diocesanism being carefully guarded against; and the elders who are associated with him in the government of the ἐκκλησία τῆς παροικίας having the name of Presbyters and a status superior to our elders. The congregation—I mean the ἐκκλησία itself—appears to be made more of than is the practice (nothing wrong, I think, in the principles) of most Presbyterians. Such, I humbly conceive, was the government of the primitive Church." But while he liked the title of bishop, if not applied to a diocesan, he expressed the strongest aversion to the title of Lords Spiritual being given to Bishops; and he refused on account of it to concur in a petition from the Presbytery to the House of Lords; because "As Lords they are not spiritual, and as spiritual they are not Lords."

He held very decided views on the *ordination* of Presbyters having been transmitted from the apostles through "the laying on of the hands of the presbytery." Not that he was anxious about the individual links in the chain, but he laid great stress on the grand historical fact. "Would you not then," I asked, "acknowledge any inherent right in the Church to constitute itself under Christ? In a company of believers cut off from the rest, as in an island, would they not have the right to appoint a ministry for themselves?" His answer was, "Your case must first suppose a chance providence." But he did not extend this view to the mere preaching of the Gospel, and of lay preaching he had no jealousy, except that it should be sound. His sentiments, however, on this point I never clearly understood. "Every man," he said, "has a right to preach, 'Let him that heareth say, Come;' but he can't oblige you to listen." But he said again, "The magistrate may preach, if he is ordained."

"The *Baptists'* way of it would never do with me," he used to say, "I would aye be coming back another time, and saying to

them, I was not a right believer yon time.
But the doctrine of the Church of England is
immersion; sprinkling is the exception." In a
depressed state he said one day to his infant
grandson, "You are a little sinner." "But he
is not responsible," it was replied. "He is
responsible," he answered, "but I hope he has
a Sponsor." This remark had no reference to
baptism, but he assigned a high place to that
ordinance; and while he held that the children
of believers are outwardly within the covenant, and therefore receive baptism as its seal,
he attached a great value to that seal, and
deeply regretted its unavoidable want. That
want has already been noticed in a short-lived
child of his own, of whom he said, "I can trust
even for my unbaptized infant." He spoke
strongly of the indelible effect of baptism :
"The water of baptism can never be wiped
from the brow," and if followed by the refusal
of Divine grace, he added, "the most awful
thing for the impenitent must be to die with
the name of Father, Son, and Holy Ghost sealed
on the forehead."

Toward men of different religious sentiments he was singularly *tolerant*, but against
all wrong opinions touching important truths
he was invariably severe. In one of his
sermons he denounced, in no measured terms,
a volume on Practical Religion, that was
written by an eminent Dissenting minister in
England, and was popular at the time, but
which appeared to him to explain away the
necessity of the new birth in those who have

been brought up in Christian families. Naming the book, he raised his voice, and announced with great force, " I say emphatically it is a bad book." But toward all men he was tolerant and tender, both in principle and in habit, and would say, " There are often heresies of the head which are not heresies of the heart." Intolerance on the part of rulers, as he knew it in Austria, was an object of his keen resentment. Half hoping that he might be able to throw some light on the subject of toleration, which is so helplessly perplexed, I asked, " How would you state Toleration ?" But his brief and immediate answer only struck into the heart of the darkness—" My difficulty in it is, that toleration implies the exercise of Royal Supremacy in things spiritual."

UNION OF UNENDOWED CHURCHES.

At the commencement of the negotiations for Union his state was one of absorbed interest and extreme concern ; neither of opposition nor concurrence, but of the deepest anxiety. After the Assembly of 1863 I put to him the not unthoughtful question—" What do you think of the Union ?" His reply was such as to pain and confound me at the time, and to arrest any further interrogation on the subject for months, or rather for years. He drew himself up with an indignation and sternness, such as he occasionally assumed in denouncing a great evil, and as to one who had committed an offence, he said to me, " What do I think of the Union? What a question is that to ask! That is not a question to be answered off-hand; it involves many considerations." Voluntaryism in its full development he looked upon as a more serious error than Erastianism, of which he could speak with sarcastic pleasantry : " Poor Erastus ! a physician ! what did he know about it ?" From the time that the proposed Union had assumed a definite form he strenuously resisted it on the ground that, although our Church by entering into it would not deny, she would cease to declare, the doctrine that it is a nation's duty to confess and establish the true religion ; and of this doctrine he said, " It is one of the great principles of all religion, natural and revealed ; it was held even by the heathen." The scriptural foundation of the doctrine he held to be unassailable, but the view of the nation's duty belonging to natural religion was the one that he oftenest insisted on ; holding that the magistrate, as the minister of God, was bound to uphold national religion under the obligation of natural law.

Of all the brethren on either side he was one of the most earnest in the controversy, and he was prepared to make any sacrifice for what he held to be momentous truth. But with all his decision of judgment and tension of feeling on the subject, his love to the many brethren who differed from him was unchanged ; he regarded them with unabated feelings of brotherhood, affection, and esteem. His state of mind through a trying conflict presented, in a manner rarely seen on earth, a most beautiful embodying of the words: " Love suffereth long and is kind, is not easily provoked, thinketh no evil, beareth all things, believeth all things, hopeth all things ; love never faileth."

THE FUTURE.

" Our times," he said, "were the fathers' prophetic themes" (1 Pet. i. 10-12); but toward the future of the church and the world not mere reserve but absolute silence was his constant attitude, with one single exception. On Prophecy he would never be prevailed upon to speak ; I never heard him utter a single thought upon the subject. This remarkable reserve was not from underrating the Old Testament. Moses, the Psalms, and the Prophets were his continual study ; and he once set himself to the great but loving task of committing the whole Hebrew Bible to memory. Nor did it arise from any aversion to inquiries on Bible subjects not essential to personal salvation. He had even tried to make out the difference between the instantaneous action of Spirit and the rapid movement of the glorified body, by the time that elapsed between Christ's ascension from the Mount of Olives and the outpouring of the Spirit at Pentecost, on the supposition that the descent of the Spirit was immediate after Christ's appearance at the Father's right hand.

But with all his Hebrew lore, so replete with the future, and with all his spirit of speculation, he was strangely but resolutely dumb both on Old Testament prophecy and on any event, such as the slaying of the witnesses, foretold in the Book of Revelation. He must often have thought on these subjects, but he had evidently never formed any scheme of prophetic interpretation that satisfied himself. Commonly it was impossible to propose any topic of inquiry which he had not investigated; but much as he liked to talk, he seldom cared to speak when he had not to some extent made up his own mind.

This extreme reserve on the prospects of the Church in general, rendered the one subject on which he broke through it the more strongly marked. That single subject was the national conversion of Israel, and the essential place allotted to their conversion in the salvation of the world. There was no part of Revelation which he held more firmly, but it was under the aspect of promise rather than of prophecy; and his hope for Israel rested not on the more prophetical parts either of the Old or the New Testament, but mainly on the eleventh chapter of the Epistle to the Romans. Their restoration to their own land he probably expected; but it is not included in that chapter, and I never heard him speak of it. He had no sympathy with those who count Israel only one among the many nations of the earth; but held that the human family still retains the two great divisions of Jew and Gentile. What is declared in that chapter, or in other passages within the like limits, seemed to contain the length and the breadth of his defined and positive creed for the future of this earth.

But this limited prophetic creed he held with a tenacity and an earnestness in proportion to its brevity and the fewness of its articles. For the Jews he had an intense and a life-long love. They were to him "beloved for the fathers' sakes" and for their own, and he could not endure the supposition that they are now cast off. He would often say, " Hath God cast away his people? God forbid." For the Gentiles, he held that all our standing is still through Israel, and our engrafting into the stock of Abraham, and that for our own sakes we must remember them and seek their salvation. In reference to those who were disposed to neglect them for what they reckoned more hopeful work among the heathen, he said with indignation : " 'Boast not against the branches ; thou bearest not the root, but the root thee.' We had better not give up Abraham ; we lose our own standing if we let Abraham go.'"

This reserve or apparent abstinence, as regards the more prophetic portions of Scripture, is no contradiction to what has been previously stated of his reverence for every word of the Bible ; and was indeed one of his ways of exercising and showing that reverence. He loved the whole Bible, but never professed to understand it all : and what he did not understand he refrained from attempting to explain. In his own mind he must have had many thoughts about the future, but he would speak of nothing as the mind of God except where he felt that he found a solid footing in his Word.

In connexion with his all but entire reserve regarding the future of the Church on earth, and notwithstanding what has already been related of his lively hope of heaven, it may be noted that the future in another state did not seem to occupy quite so large a place in his conversation or in his preaching as in most men of equal grace; and when he did speak of it, it was with a very immediate reference to the past and the present. Occasionally he made remarks that showed he had thought most intensely on the subject, and that the eternal future was habitually in his mind; and in his dejections, the loss of heaven and the fear of hell were only too vivid before him, and he gave free utterance to his fears. But with the exception of the mansions in the Father's house, to which I have previously referred, I seldom remember him either taking a text or dwelling at any length on the future world, either of weal or woe. Even that sermon with all its vividness, seeming to translate you into heaven, took no colouring tint from the more prophetic or more figurative parts of Scripture ; not even such as " the Lamb leading them by fountains of living waters ;" and when you thought it over, it was throughout rather the preparation of the men for the mansions than of the mansions for the men, or at least the character of the man was much more its subject than the character of the mansion. So of the angel whom he wished to see, the scene before him was the dark agony in the garden with the bright messenger ministering; and so in the study from the summit of the hill, it was not heaven foreseen from earth, but earth to be remembered in heaven.

He once said to me with the liveliest interest, " I would like to preach from that text, ' After that He was seen of above five hundred brethren at once.' " The opening of this attractive scene would have been exactly his description of heaven, yet not of the future which he seemed to shrink from attempting, but of heaven as then actually let down to earth : The centre of all, the Lord Jesus, whom he never wearied contemplating; then Jesus in his risen beauty and glory; and Jesus seen with open face by an adoring and admiring multitude of surrounding saints.

His thoughts were much occupied with the Judgment, and he would repeat with great force, and with application both to saints and sinners, the words of the Lord Jesus, " I say unto you, my friends, Fear him, who after he hath killed, hath power to cast into hell; yea, I say unto you, Fear him." The atheistic idea of man's existence ending with this present life was loathsome to him, even when he believed it; and the devil once cast out never returned. Yet his thoughts seemed to turn to the great Judge more than to the great Day, and to Christ crucified on Calvary and now at the Father's right hand more than to his coming again in glory. There was in him a cast of the Old Testament saint, with Christ in all his fulness, not added, but occupying the centre and filling all. The division of man's existence into the present and the eternal was perhaps not quite so broad with him as it is with many. He seemed to think more on man in his entire existence, and in his relations to God the Judge and Christ the Redeemer. In criticism on a remark which I had made in preaching, that "The narrow way throughout all its course runs close by the brink of eternity," he said, "Well, I am not sure. I think I have sometimes had much of the presence of the Spirit when the future eternity was not so much in my mind." Yet he had it very fully in his own way, and a great many years before his death he said to me, "Well, if I were sure of heaven, there is nothing I would like better than to depart and be with Christ."

O

CHAPTER X.

THOUGHTS ON PREACHING.

The best preaching is : Believe on the Lord Jesus Christ, and keep
the Ten Commandments.—J. D.

Of his own preaching in Glasgow Dr. Duncan
remarked at a subsequent period,—" I was a
very popular preacher till I began to preach
on the work of the Spirit, then the church
grew thin." This he gave as an indication
of the natural aversion to whatever is most
spiritual. But on another occasion, at a later
period, when it had been suggested in our
Presbytery to recommend ministers to preach
specially on the work of the Spirit, he said to
me,—" I doubt the wisdom of the proposal. I
think that no extensive awakening has ever
been produced by preaching on the work of
the Spirit, but rather by awakening the conscience and setting forth Christ. The best
preaching is, Believe on the Lord Jesus Christ,
and keep the Ten Commandments."

"Preaching is the delivery of a message"
was one of his favourite sayings. "One felt
that he was so distinctively taught of the
Spirit of the Lord, that his sayings, aided by

their epigrammatic terseness and point, stuck fast in the conscience and memory, in their measure, like texts of Scripture. Many of his remarks bore the mark, as was said of Samuel Johnson's, of 'attrition in his nightly mind.' They had long been accurately formed and polished, and came forth from time to time, in almost the same terms. His frequent illustration of the true function of ministers, not to fabricate but to deliver a message, κηρύσσειν τὸ εὐαγγέλιον (to proclaim the good tidings), was a notable example of this habit." [14]

"The Gospel," he said again, "is a light, and when faithfully preached it radiates. God spoke corporeal light out of darkness, but moral light is not produced by a word, but by His own shining in our hearts, 2 Cor. iv. 6, 7. We have the light of Jehovah's countenance shining in that of the Messiah, and from that shining into the hearts of his servants, and from them through the ministration of the Gospel in the hearts of sinners. Besides light there is power, first set forth as illumination, and then as a treasure (ver. 7). This change in the metaphor is perhaps connected with the idea of the Jews, that the first light was not the ordinary daylight, but a distinct substance which was treasured up for the just in future times : the treasured light. The Gospel is enlightening and enriching ; the light of the glory of God in the face of Jesus Christ, being shined by the power of God into our hearts, that we may hold up that light to others, while the power of causing that light to shine into their hearts is reserved to Himself. The Gospel is needed equally by every man; it is adapted to every man; by God's appointment it is to be preached to every man under heaven. Christ is a needed, a suitable, an accessible Saviour. Christ has not given power to any man, be he who he may, to dispense Gospel blessings; but the men sent by Christ are required to point to Christ as an accessible Saviour in whom there is redemption through his blood." [17]

" Preach the antinomies of truth, and carry each out as far as it is possible to carry it. But don't attempt to reconcile them. These two lines will meet if produced far enough. But if I try to make them meet, I give one or other of them a twist, and so reduce it from being a straight line. If the stones of an arch were to become animated and speak, the stones on the right hand would say, ' Right-hand pressure is right pressure;' and the stones on the left hand would say, ' Left-hand pressure is right pressure;' but by pressing in opposite directions they keep up the keystone of the arch." [15]

On the external part of preaching he made an observation fitted to be useful to ministers for a large portion of their people : " I used to care only for the thoughts in a sermon, but now that I am getting old I am the better of some physical energy in the preacher; I find it helps to keep the intellect going."

ON PREACHERS.

He discerned with a keen subtlety the characteristics of preachers, and told them with a
singular felicity. There were few things that
interested him more than criticism of this
kind. He was a most attentive and devout
hearer of the Word of God ; he listened with
the receptivity of a little child, and with the
closest self-application, yet his critical faculty
could not be lulled asleep. After an able,
highly Calvinistic sermon, he would say to
your surprise, " Our friend has got afraid to
preach the gospel." Of another, of an opposite
stamp, " Very good for bringing people to
decision, but the doctrine is Wesleyan Method-
ism." After hearing an exposition of the
passage, " Jerusalem which is above is the
mother of us all," in which the preacher ex-
plained the words to mean, " Jerusalem which
is *from* above," he said, " Tell that young
minister that there is no want of prepositions
in Greek ; if Paul had meant ' from above,' he
could have said it."

Of one preacher he would say, " He wants
taste, and will always want it ; he is essentially
vulgar ;" and of another, placing him in a
widely different class, " He is quite a gentleman himself, but he has a vulgar intellect."
On a preacher whom he had heard several
times he remarked, " He has only a few Gospel
texts and thoughts from the New Testament ;
what does he make of the Old ? That will
never meet the wants of the whole man, and

of his state in this world; we must have the Bible." A minister earnestly asked him for a text. He gave him one, and another, and another, but was met with the constant reply, "I've preached on all these, can you give no other?" "Let me think," he said, and walking up and down for a little he answered, "If ye know these things, happy are ye if ye do them." "Thank you, that will do excellently."

He would often strike off the characters of men in a single sentence or expression in a way that was extremely interesting, either because it presented them in quite a new light, or because it happily hit what was most characteristic. At the funeral of one of our elders he made a remark, which was instantly felt to be the most apt that could have been offered, although it had occurred to no one else. He said of the deceased: "He had this token of being a child of God, he was 'a lover of good men.'"

When he had once formed the image of a man in his own conception, he was not easily induced to alter it, even where it was too ideal to be accurate. After passing a high and very definite eulogy on a young preacher whom he had heard, he was told that he was mistaken in his estimate, because the young man was vain of his talents. He replied, "That may be true of him as he is known to you, but the young preacher of my charity is such as I have described him."

If he had been much edified by a sermon, the spiritual benefit rather moved him the more to correct any defect by a kindly remark, doctrinal, practical, or critical : " A very good man, and he gave us a most excellent sermon, but he has very few vocables ; you should advise him to get more English words." A mere store of vocables, however, apart from acquaintance with the structure of a language gave him no contentment ; and of one biblical author he remarked : " He knows the vocables of a number of languages, but he does not know any language." His own " vocabulary " was incomparably rich ; no other man seemed to possess such a treasure of words. " Will Shakespeare," he said, " is after all about the best English we have ; if I were to begin again, I think I would take him for my model." His own English took its range from the tersest Saxon, which he liked best and used most, and traversed all through to the other verge of Anglicised Latin. He had a want of fluency in speech ; chiefly, perhaps, because he shrank instinctively from combining words to embody only a principal idea, however good, without each part being stamped with a distinct value of its own. But he owned a boundless wealth of language, and nothing would induce him to use any word but the one that exactly fitted his thought. On hearing in a resolution read in our Assembly the expression " vital error," he asked, " What kind of error is that ? truth is vital, but what is a vital error ? it should be mortal error." Another in making such a correction would have suggested fatal or deadly error. Neither of these, however, would have reached the precision of his mind, because the one was Saxon and the other was not the exact contrary to vital; but "mortal" clothed his thought both in meaning and in form.

This sensitively critical precision pervaded all his speaking and all his hearing. Even when his speech gushed in torrents, he must have the very word that was made to express the shade of thought; Scotch if there was no English for it; or if necessary some portentous "vocable" derived from the dead tongues. In listening, a misapplied word never escaped his notice, and he could not refrain from correcting it. At the close of a service in church I had given out the lines :—

> " His presence fills each heart with joy,
>   Tunes every mouth to sing :
> By day, by night, the sacred courts
>   With glad Hosannahs ring."

On coming down from the pulpit he said to me, "There are no Hosannahs in heaven;" meaning that our Hosannahs are there changed into Halleluiahs.

On the preaching of Jonathan Edwards, he said, "His doctrine is all application, and his application all doctrine." But the most graphic of his conversational criticisms on the pulpit, was his comparison of two great preachers, Dr. Chalmers and Dr. Gordon; but his voice and action added a vividness which we cannot transfer by the pen. "They were both one-ideaed preachers; but I used to compare the one to a showman and the other to a hunts-man. Dr. Chalmers was the showman, and

his idea was the showman's box, which he set
down before you and said, 'Here's the idea.'
Then he took it up in his hands, and turned
it, and showed it in every possible way : ' This
is the top of it, and this is the bottom ; this is
its front, and this is its back ; this is its right
side, this is the left ; this is the outside and
this is the inside : so there you have the whole
idea.' Dr. Gordon was the huntsman, and his
idea was the fox which he asked you to help
him to catch : ' You cannot see it yet, but we
shall search the thicket and make sure to find
it. It is somewhere in this cover ; let us first
beat for it on the right, next let us turn and
beat the bushes on the left. It is not in either,
let us now beat straight in front. Sniff ! sniff !
we have got on the scent, we shall soon catch
it now, it must be very near—ho, there it is
at last ! look, that is it ! the idea :'—and he
closed the book just the moment *before* you
had caught it." The same thought has been
otherwise expressed, that "the idea was in the
sentence after the last."

After the death of Dr. Gordon, to whose
clear and earnest teaching of the way of life
not a few teachers of others were deeply indebted, Dr. Duncan in conducting an ordinary
service in church began in a loud voice, and
said with a singular majesty and force, " Know
ye not that there is a Prince and a great man
fallen this day in Israel ?" He added no comment ; yet more effectually than by a long
oration did these few words, as he spoke them,
set forth the prince-like grandeur of the dead,

and awaken at once admiration for his character and sorrow for Israel's loss.

"There is," he said, "a sort of preaching in a biblical orthodox way which sets everybody asleep.—I want my religious teacher to give me the nut as it came from God, and to leave it to myself and to God to crack it between us." [5]

At the close of a sermon on the words, "The peace of God which passeth all understanding shall keep (*Gr.* shall keep as by soldiers in a fortress) your hearts and minds through Christ Jesus," [3] he came up to the preacher with his own summary of the text, clinching it with his sharp incisive "What ?" —his constant mode of eliciting assent to a sentence which in his own judgment was both justly conceived and rightly worded. His beautiful paraphrase of the text was this : "Christ Jesus is the garrison and Peace is the sentinel."

MISCELLANEOUS THOUGHTS.

If we have not got a cross, alas! we may conclude that we have not got Christ, for it is the first of his gifts.

Can you be happy just by thinking that God is happy?

It requires an infinite intellect to comprehend the infinite ; therefore God can be known as He is to Himself alone.

Sin and misery : It is not, The *cruel* God loves misery, but the *righteous* God loves righteousness.

God's law is not merely the expression of God's arbitrary will, it is the expression of his moral perfections.

God will multiply to pardon; but modify and take down his law ! never.

A holy God and an unholy sinner, an angry God and a guilty sinner, would not make a happy heaven together.

If one sin destroyed man's moral nature, every sin strengthens man's depravity.

God needs to do a great deal *to* sinners, in order to turn them ; but God is requiring nothing *of* sinners but that they return.

Sinning is not a rare thing, but repenting is; sinning not rare, but taking a right view of sin, saying right about sin, that is rare.

Every sin will be adequately punished; blessed be God, not every *sinner*.

You don't make Christ a present when you give him your heart, you only give him that which He has already bought.

The Lord's Prayer: that is God's order in prayer. (God first.) The believer often puts himself first; God may pardon the dislocation, but he does not approve of it.

In ghosts I neither believe nor disbelieve: how can I come to a conclusion when I have no data? Some people must come to a conclusion about everything. I believe that most of the stories told are great nonsense; at the same time I am a very sceptical unbeliever.— M. R.

Is man active or passive in regeneration? He is both; he is active *about* it, and passive *in* it.[2]

There is no doubting in faith; there may be much doubting in the believer.

Christ has a threefold work; a work for us, a work in us, and a work by us.

All sin is damning in its nature.

Fasting is a duty, an extraordinary one.

There is nothing but Christ between us and hell; and, thanks be to God, *we need* nothing else.

In the prospect of judgments the Divine call

is, "Enter into thy chambers," *i.e.* To your closets, gentlemen.

The revivals, as Dr. Cunningham said, may leave some thousands converted.

The offer of Christ more than makes up for the fall.[9]

Cain was a Deist, that is, an impenitent Theist.

In Noah we have the first account of justification by grace.[13]

I thank God for the removal of sickness; but I have been able to give thanks for sickness, for health, for light, for darkness, for the hiding of God's face.

"God doth fail *me* never:" oh the "*me* never:" the unchangeable God giving strength to the fainting heart and flesh.

How wonderful to reconcile these two: God's greatness and perfect happiness without the creature at all, and yet he is said to be grieved: "Grieve not the Spirit of God." Oh how sad to grieve the Comforter!

Beware of religion without God. Many are satisfied with a religion without God in the present day; but that only which comes from God will lead to God.—A.

"In the beginning" puts an end to all cosmogonies. Plato mounted as far as any one to an architect of the universe. With him God and "prima mater" were eternal existences. Judaism and Christianity are distinct from Heathenism in its two forms, Pantheism and Dualism. Pantheism, with its emanations flowing from it, afforded no ground for moral science, as it gave way to Polytheism. The τὸ κάλον κἄγαθον of Plato involved a moral discrimination; and so the ὕλη was accounted bad. But this was Dualism, from which arose Manicheeism. The religion of Israel was that of a Holy God, and therefore absolutely and infinitely distinct from others.

Sin is spiritual nakedness; shame is connected with conscious guilt; because of the external loathing of the body by God, coats of skin were made to cover the body.

That which has become the byword of all un-Christians must be the very core of Christianity.

The Law was imperfect, but had within itself a perfect unity.

A bad Demiurge (Maker) could never have made me with such a conscience.

Law is not itself eternal, because there are no eternal subjects; but the principle of law is eternal, because it is a necessity of God's being. Man was placed under a positive law: it is difficult to conceive how sin could enter under a mere moral law. Man was subjected to the law: Thou shalt, Thou shalt not; and not to the law: A being B, B is not C; B being C, A is not B. Even in the case of the angels, the origin of sin may be traced to some positive law of God.

God probably appeared to man in a human form. "Enoch walked with God," which appears to mean that God assumed a visible form, and that He and Enoch often had walks together; that the Spirit penetrated into the material by a theophany, such as in the bush.

Our first parents must have seen a "minimum quid" in the promise, but the "quantum" we do not know. A suffering but conquering Deliverer is promised.

Here we are, with the heavens above our heads. What are we? Men. How came we to be men? What is man? how came he to be? and to be as he is? We are on the earth, and the beasts can't ask any questions; the heavens are above us, and the eagle soaring into them can't ask any questions. "In the beginning God created"—Man is God's image on earth; man, the divinely-formed microcosm, of the dust of the earth and the breath of God. Dust connects him with this earth, with the whole solar system, with the whole mass of matter, which, so far as we can judge, is a unit. We differ from it πλάσματι (by formation): God put his *hand* to us; He made the rest by his *word*. We were made in Adam before he sinned; we are therefore connected with God and with the whole world of spirits.

David says, "Cast me not from thy sight," implying, "For I have sinned like Cain, and thou mightest do so."

The question of the different nationalities will stir the earth likely until the millennium. "Go ye into all nations" acknowledges them. Kossuth accuses anti-nationalists of impiety. "Before him shall be gathered all nations."

Don't make faith a cloak for sin. Be sure

of coming to Christ : Be sure of abiding in
Christ : Be sure of bringing forth fruit to
Christ. [5]

The man who has no more in him that what
belongs to him understands not the things of
the Spirit of God : man who has only a human
soul receiveth not the things spoken.

As a brute beast cannot know the things of
a psychic (natural) man, no more can a psychic
(natural) man know the things of a pneumatic
(spiritual) man. It is beyond the power of an
apostle to make a pneumatic man of him, for
he holds the apostle himself a babbler; but
this man alone will receive the things of the
Spirit.[1]

The man who would rest content with God's
mercy at some future time, is the man who is
content to rest without it.

All the intercourse which God has had with
man has been through Jesus Christ.

The *guilt* of sin is the product of two things :
First, of sin which is the transgression of the
law ; and, Second, of justice which is the main-
tenance of the law. The particular aspect of
sin to justice and of justice to sin is what is
properly the guilt of sin. The guilt of sin is
neither the bare act nor the punishment of it,
but something between them.

A man cannot be justified but as a condemned sinner ; and he cannot be justified at
the bar of God if he is merely condemned at
the bar of God, and is not also condemned at

the bar of conscience. The work of the law must be accomplished in every man in shutting his mouth and bringing him in guilty in his own esteem. The question which suggests itself to a man awakened to see himself described by the law of God is : Can there be a salvation which answers the demands of the law ? [17]

It is a monstrous thing, the *disembodied* state of a man. We are not angels, we were never made to be angels, we don't like to be angels, we won't continue to be angels. God has put an instinct within us against it, for the idea of the man is body and spirit.

God filled the world with Man : Sin filled the world with sinners. [15]

_____

NAMES OF CONTRIBUTORS.

To the contributors to this little volume I feel deeply grateful. As the simplest mode of acknowledgment I have numbered the writers in the order of their contributions as received or used, attaching a reference number to each quotation. The reference to the top of p. 87 has unfortunately been lost in transcribing ; in some instances the same notes have been sent by several contributors ; and in others the

contributors have preferred that I should withhold their names. To several of my esteemed
friends I owe very special thanks, but on balancing my debts I have found myself unable to
draw the line of my more special obligations.

1. Rev. ALEXANDER WATT, Kineff.
2. Rev. JAMES JOHNMAN, Newluce.
3. Rev. JOHN ROBERTS, Edinburgh.
4. Rev. JAMES JOHN SMITH, Shetland.
5. Rev. GEORGE REITH, Glasgow.
6. Rev. DONALD FERGUSON, Leven.
7. Rev. ROBERT BOAG WATSON, Madeira.
8. Rev. JAMES B. IRVINE, Strathkinness.
9. Rev. G. MITCHELL, Kilmadock.
10. Rev. WILLIAM OWEN ALLAN, St. Thomas.
11. Rev. JAMES DONALDSON, Ontario.
12. Rev. R. J. SANDEMAN, Edinburgh.
13. Rev. ROBERT SAUNDERS, Paisley.
14. Rev. JOHN DONALDSON, Ceres.
15. Rev. ROBERT COWAN, Perth.
16. Rev. JOHN KIPPEN, Arrochar.
17. Rev. WILLIAM BALFOUR, Edinburgh.
18. Rev. ALEXANDER TOMORY, Constantinople.
19. Rev. ROBERT SMITH, Corsock.
20. Rev. JOHN D. FISHER, Aberlemno.

The greater number of Recollections without
names are my own; the others have all been
derived from direct sources, with the single
exception (so far as I remember) of the first little
incident in p. 117, which is an old story of no
importance, but of which I never doubted the
accuracy, and which I think was told me with
the names at the time.

INDEX.

EDINBURGH : T. AND A. CONSTABLE,
PRINTERS TO THE QUEEN, AND TO THE UNIVERSITY.